PUBLISHED IN 2021 BY TITAN

© 2021 SUZY SHAW

America's Food Hub
Titangate Press

First published in 2019. Third edition.

America's Food Hub is an imprint of Titangate Press.

All inquiries, requests and correspondence about this product should be directed to the following email address:

americasfoodhub@gmail.com

ISBN: 9798747760899

British Library Cataloging in Publication Data
A catalogue record for this book is available from the British Library.
Repository XI, Domicile 23, Data Bank 2—Cooking Manuals

Library of Congress Cataloging in Publication Data
Suzy Shaw, 2019—Index 22a, Cookbooks & Household Media

Front, Interior & Back Design
By Excelsior Fonts, 1 Rockwell Ave, New York, NY, 10504

Printed in the United States of America
By Amazon and its affiliates, 410 Terry Ave, North, Seattle, WA, 98109-5210

TITANGATE PRESS
Time is Knowledge.

CONTENTS

SNACKS, DISHES & APPETIZERS

LUNCH, BRUNCH & MEALS

DESSERTS

KETO DIET 101

MISSION STATEMENT...

Your body is a machine. Therefore, it is intelligent. Millions of years of evolution means it knows exactly what it needs to survive, and this is energy. Without it, the cells which make your body you would stop working and you would die. Not to worry! Your body is smart; it has evolved many metabolic pathways to stay alive. They convert the food you eat into energy, but not just any energy, useful energy called carbohydrate (carbs); it is useful because it energizes your body. Eating carbs fuels your body with energy because carbs contain a naturally occurring sugar called glucose; your body uses it as energy. Your body is very smart; it has evolved ways to control how many carbs it uses as energy. Eating more carbs than your body uses for energy means it converts unused energy to fat and stores this fat around your body: you get fat! Do you remember your high school science class? There, you might have learned that energy can't be created nor destroyed, only exchanged from one form to another. Your body works the same; it is physical reflection of nature's intelligence. Keto is beautiful because it's where natural physical and biological laws merge to forge a rejuvenating equilibrium for your body.

So... You might be wondering what happens in the opposite situation: what if you deprive your body of carbs? Science gives us the answer. Your body uses its stored fat as energy (energy = glucose = carbs) and you lose weight. How does this work? It comes down to your liver. This important organ breaks down your body's stored fat into fatty acids, which are broken down into smaller molecules, or things, called ketones. By a simple chemical process, those ketones are absorbed through the walls of your small intestine and insulin transports them around your blood stream and supplies all the cells making up your body with energy; you stay alive! This process is called ketosis. Simple, isn't it? Well, this is where the keto diet works. Following a keto diet means your body stays in ketosis for a long time and you lose weight by eating keto approved foods: foods low in carbs and high in healthy fats. The many recipes included in the following pages will help your body fall into the natural stasis of ketosis and this healing process will transform you into a new you in the most affordable, quick and easy way imaginable! In this new edition, you'll find...

- ✓ **Affordable ingredients:** save money with budget friendly meals.
- ✓ **5-ingredients or less:** cut expensive and hard to find ingredients.
- ✓ **Easy to find ingredients:** find recipe ingredients easily online and at your local grocery store.
- ✓ **Quick & easy recipes:** cook using simple, tasty and wholesome ingredients.
- ✓ **Nutritional information:** keep track of your keto macros.
- ✓ **30-day keto meal plan:** lose up to 7 lbs every week.
- ✓ **Servings:** cook right-sized food portions for your meal plan.
- ✓ **Shopping lists:** buy only the ingredients needed for your meal plan.
- ✓ **Cooking times:** save time and stress around the kitchen.
- ✓ **Keto diet guide:** master ketosis and lose weight fast!
- ✓ **Highly rated recipes:** enjoy only the most popular hand-selected recipes.

Do you want to lose weight on a keto diet but don't know how? Don't worry! Everyone, even Amazon, knows that keto is confusing, especially if you love splurging on junk food! So... this best-selling 'go-to' keto diet resource will teach you how to not only start, but love, keto. Featuring an easily digestible keto guide, meal plan, shopping lists and pages upon pages of award-winning recipes, from breakfast, brunch and lunch through to snacks, side dishes and desserts, you'll smash your weight loss goal in the most affordable, quick and easy way possible...

... Shed the flab & look fab! Get that healthy body you have always dreamt of!

The keto diet, also called the ketogenic, low-carb and LCHF diet, is a low-carbohydrate, high-fat diet. Science tells us that keto foods are healthier than traditional diet foods on the Atkins diet. This book dispels the myths surrounding the keto diet by promoting a simple, budget-friendly, yet result-oriented diet plan based around a metabolic state called ketosis, offering many health benefits like improving appetite, cutting cholesterol and blood pressure, reducing stroke, epilepsy and Alzheimer's risk and reversing diabetes. Inside the pages of this cookbook, you'll love a tasty variety of sweet, savory, salty, crispy and craveable meals, as well as a wonderful selection of traditional and modern recipes like...

American Pancakes, Donuts, Crispy Bacon & Eggs, Jarlsberg Lunch Omelet, Oh so good' Salad, 'I Love Bacon', 'No Potato' Shepherd's Pie, Dijon Halibut Steak, Keto Fat Bombs, 'Nearly' Pizza, Cheesecake Cups, Chocolate Chip Cookies, Ballin' Berry Layer Cake, Chocolate Pudding, Strawberry Shakes... And so much more goodness!

Welcome to the low-carb revolution... It's a fabulous lifestyle!

Warmest Regards,

Suzy Shaw

Nutritionist & Diet Coach
America's Food Hub

KETO EXPLAINED

A ketogenic, or keto, diet is a low-carb high-fat (LCHF) diet and stands out among popular regimens. Unlike many diet trends and fads, it's straightforward and easy to follow once you get to grips with it. The diet is based on reducing the amount of carbs you eat and replacing them with healthy fat. High carb foods cause your body to produce insulin and glucose; it is the sensitive interaction between them, which is described in detail later, which controls a weight loss process called ketosis. So, your success on the keto diet depends on how successful you are with managing ketosis, and this depends on how disciplined you are in limiting your high-carb food intake.

- **Glucose:** A simple sugar that converts energy from the food we eat to fuel our body.
- **Insulin:** A hormone our pancreas secretes to transport glucose (energy) through our bloodstream to our cells.

Since the dawn of civilization in East Africa, glucose has been a human's primary source of energy; it is what we use to fuel our body, fight off competition, evolve and stay alive! On a regular diet today, especially one followed by a modern human, glucose converts to fat in our bodies at a rate faster than what occurred in the bodies of our distant ancestors: we are larger than them, physically. Indeed, science tells us that modern humans living today are eating too many high carbohydrate foods. This excess carb consumption means our bodies are storing glucose in the fatty deposits around our body more than it should or has done historically: we are fat! Fortunately, we humans have evolved an intelligent body. Our body doesn't use this excess supply of glucose caused by a generic, unhealthy Westernized diet as energy because it has no need to if we're constantly eating foods high in carbs. So, our body doesn't need it and simply stores it away as fat to be used when our dietary habit changes: a change on the keto diet that we call ketosis. Science tells us that carbs are our number-one source of energy, and while this may be true, carbs do not come without their drawbacks. The keto diet eliminates these problems by substituting carbs with healthy fats and some protein. But the amount of carbs we substitute on the diet depends on our dietary preference and which variation of the diet we follow.

KETO CALORIE BUDGET

Importantly, the keto diet is based on the nutritional science of a daily calorie budget, which varies for male and females. Energy, our body's fuel, is measured in calories. Humans consume calories every day, whether we know it or not. Food, such as carbs, contains calories: calories provide energy. This is true whether you're following a keto diet or not. Science tells us two things:
1. The keto diet prescribes a calorie intake lower than one on a non-keto diet.
2. This calorie intake varies between men and women.

The American Medical Association recommends the following general daily calorie intake for men and women following a keto diet. Note, this is a general recommendation and doesn't consider your weight, height, BMI and overall medical history and condition. So, you should consult your physician prior to starting one of the keto diets below. They will calculate a daily calorie budget most suitable for you. Alternatively, you can use an online calculator to do the calculation yourself, although I don't recommend this option because my experience suggests that most people calculate it incorrectly.

GENDER	DAILY CALORIE BUDGET
Male	1200
Female	1000

The science behind the calorie intake is that the amount of energy stored inside your body is equal to the energy in minus energy out. This can be represented mathematically by the following equation:

ENERGY STORED = ENERGY IN - ENERGY OUT

This relationship implies that if you, as an active human being, burn more calories by doing physical work such as exercise, regulating core bodily function/processes (staying alive), than you intake daily, you will lose weight. This is the traditional weight loss model, but it is basic. Translated to the keto diet, your focus and priority whilst on the diet is to minimize 'energy in' (by limiting calorie intake) to your body so that ketosis forces it to burn calories from its existing 'energy stored'. So, your focus on the diet is to manipulate the energy that comes into your body by changing what you eat: by avoiding high-carb foods. But, this is where it might get a little complicated: the difference between keto and a normal diet is that keto focuses on intentionally splitting this daily calorie budget across three common macronutrient groups: carbs, proteins and fats. In other words, each version of the keto diet apportions a specific percentage to each group. So, every form of keto diet, and there are four main types described below, is based on this fundamental science of a daily calorie budget. Each type must have a specific calorie budget assigned to it for the diet to work and this budget is divided differently across the three macro food groups, depending on which type of diet you choose to follow. Without one, the diet would not work; it is what all knowledge of the diet rests on and is top of the list of your 'things to do before starting a keto diet'. The four main types of keto diet are:

1. **Standard Ketogenic Diet (SKD):** This is the most popular form. It is the one highly recommended by nutritionists and advertised online. It is based on splitting your daily calorie budget into a macronutrient ratio of 75% fat, 20% protein and 5% carbs.
2. **High-Protein Ketogenic Diet:** This involves eating more protein and is based on splitting your daily calorie budget into a macronutrient ratio of 60% fat, 35% protein and 5% carbs.
3. **Targeted Ketogenic Diet (TKD):** This a good choice for athletes who use up their glycogen reserves quickly and involves consuming more carbs than on a SKD.
4. **Cyclical Ketogenic Diet (CKD):** Your carb intake varies on this variety. You dedicate two days a week to high-carb consumption and five days being ketogenic: low-carb intake.

While a standard keto diet is encouraged amongst beginners, it's important to also consider the other three, especially if one better fits your medical history, lifestyle and body. I recommend all beginners start with the SKD. Many keto dieters achieve excellent results with it right off the bat—some of them exceed expectations! Usually, though, it takes most people a little time to adapt to its challenges. Starting something new is not an easy thing for us humans to do and the keto diet is no exception. All types of keto diet require patience and perseverance. Be careful, though, a lot of misinformation surrounds it, some of which is described in this book. So, what does this mean? In a nutshell, it means that you will eat less food on keto and therefore fewer calories. Your body uses your fat stores, since you're naturally restricting carbs and you lose weight!

KETO HISTORY

20TH CENTURY—PRESENT

THE keto diet is not new. Would you believe that it dates as far back as antiquity? Fasting, which is what the keto diet evolved from, was first recommended by the Ancient Greek physician Hippocrates as a method for controlling seizures. Fast-forward 2500 years and

"All Disease Begins In The **Gut**."
- Hippocrates

the keto modern form of the keto diet dates back to the 1920s. In fact, it predates most other diets on the market today. Like Hippocratic medicine, it was first intended as a treatment for epilepsy. Rollin Woodyatt, an American endocrinologist, found that periods of fasting helped minimize seizures in his patients. Why? Reducing daily calorific intake also induces ketosis, as well as restricting carbs, as decades of science suggests. Ketosis stabilizes neuron function because it reduces the amount of glucose in the human brain: glucose is responsible for epileptic seizures. So, less glucose causes fewer epileptic seizures to occur over time. The human liver is what reduces blood glucose by producing three water-soluble compounds, β-hydroxybutyrate, acetoacetate

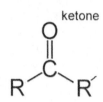

and acetone. These compounds are what Woodyatt later defined in his 1921 research, *The Threshold of Ketogenesis*, as ketones. This was a ground-breaking medical discovery at the time. It meant that the keto diet was a doctor's preferred treatment option and was an effective precursor to the various medications that were later developed to combat epilepsy, such as insulin injections. Still, even today, 20 to 30 percent of epilepsy sufferers still find the diet more effective than medication.

This scientific discovery laid the foundations for a tsunami of medical research on keto and its potential as a medicinal treatment for a broader range of health problems. In the early 20th century, American writer Bernarr Macfadden advocated fasting as a means of improving a human's overall health and well-being. His student, osteopath Hugh Conklin, subsequently introduced fasting to alleviate epilepsy. Conklin believed that fasting for 18 to 25 days could completely rid the body of the 'toxin' thought to cause epileptic seizures. His research culminated in the first translation of ketogenic principles into a dietary context: the 'water diet'. Twenty percent of his patients prescribed this diet became seizure-free, while a further 50 percent manifested a significant improvement in their condition. The water diet continued unabated into the pre and post war period where it was prescribed to soldiers and patients suffering from PTSD. The American physician, Dr Russell Wilder, of the renowned Mayo Clinic, Minnesota, United States, built on Woodyatt's work and coined the term 'ketogenic diet'. Wilder's science indicates that limited carbs and excess fat increases ketones in the blood and his further research suggests that Medium-chain Triglycerides, which are found in fats and foods such as palm and coconut oil, produce even more ketones per unit of energy. So, this discovery sparked the emphasize of a keto diet as a high fat diet, as well as a low-carb one.

The final development came in the 1960s. Peter Huttenlocher, a paediatric nutritionist, discovered 60 percent of a daily calorific intake to come from MCTs across a wide variety of oils, which meant more protein and carbohydrate could be consumed than on the classic version of the diet; thus, the high protein keto diet was birthed. This meant that a wider meal choice was now available to patients. By 2007, the keto diet is available in 45 countries, and less restrictive variants, such as the Atkins diet, are in use, particularly among children and adults. Do these discoveries and their science mean a ketogenic option is better than an artificial man-made treatment? This is an interesting question and one which raises many philosophical and ethical implications in our modern and constantly changing 21st century society.

THE HORMONE LINK

DIETARY SCIENCE

TO understand how the low-carb lifestyle of the keto diet works, you must understand its dietary science. There are four interacting areas: (i) insulin; (ii) glucagon; (iii) insulin resistance and diabetes; (iv) ketosis.

INSULIN

Science tells us that weight loss on keto is about insulin: insulin must be kept low. In other words, the lower your insulin level is, the more weight you will lose. What is insulin? Insulin is a hormone, or chemical messenger, that your pancreas releases, or secretes, into your circulatory system: bloodstream. This happens shortly after you eat food that contains sugar: glucose. Insulin breaks down glucose, amongst other things like amino acids and fatty acids, in the foods you eat. You can think of insulin as a quality control inspector: it fixes itself onto cells all around your body and decides when to open them up to let insulin flow inside. Glucose is important because it supplies those cells with energy. If there is too much glucose trying to flow inside the cells, a bottleneck occurs, and this is where your liver comes into play; it will convert the excess glucose to glycogen. Insulin transports and stores the remaining glucose inside fat cells called adipocytes. If more of those cells build up, you become fat. So, a low-carb lifestyle is all about low blood insulin levels. Interesting, right?

GLUCAGON

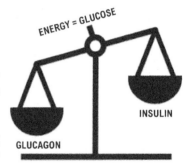

Nature made your body; it will operate to naturalistic principles. Physical science tells us that when two objects interact, they exert opposite forces on each other. Biological science tells us that glucagon is the opposite of insulin. You can visualize this balance as an equilibrium on a set of scales. If your blood sugar level dips below 75 miligrams per 100 millilitres, gluconeogenesis (the production of glucagon in the pancreas) occurs and it converts glucose inside your liver back into free glucose, meaning your body has the energy it requires to operate: to stay alive. Hypoglycaemia occurs when this balancing process between glucagon: glucose does not occur, perhaps due to a medical condition such as diabetes. Eating high-carb foods can disrupt this sensitive glucagon: glucose relationship and stop ketosis, meaning your chance of weight loss on the keto diet is greatly reduced. What does this mean? If there is insulin inside your body, there will be fat too. The trick is to keep your carb consumption low (under 25 grams per day) to keep your blood insulin level low, which means your body burns fat for energy via ketosis instead of glucose in high-carb foods.

INSULIN RESISTANCE & DIABETES

Science recognizes two types of diabetes: type I and type II. Type I diabetes is when your pancreas cannot make insulin, whereas type II is when it has resistance to it and is thought to be a 'lifestyle' disease. Their exact cause is a complicated interplay between genetics and environment, though isn't well understood. The inability of your pancreas to secrete insulin causes glucose to accumulate in your bloodstream, causing hyperglycaemia and the visual sign of diabetes such as neuropathy. The cause of this is largely uncertain but it is thought that a high-carb diet causes too much glucose in your blood, causing cells to lose their 'receptors' and prevent the 'neutralizing' insulin from entering inside.

PATHOLOGY: TESTING YOUR BLOOD

You should regularly get your bloods done on a LCHF / keto diet.

BLOOD READING	IDEAL RANGE
HDL The quantity of 'good' cholesterol in your blood.	> 1.7 mmol/L
LDL The quantity of 'bad' cholesterol in your blood. Unlike HDL where the quantity matters, the molecule size of LDL is important. Large sizes are preferred. Lower sizes indicate a higher risk of cancer.	3—6 mmol/L
Triglycerides A high quantity of triglycerides in your blood decreases weight loss.	0.5—0.9 mmol/L
Glucose A sugar derived from carbohydrate used by your body as energy.	3.5/5 mmol/L
Insulin Insulin is a hormone that moves glucose from your blood into the cells for energy and storage.	< 5.5 mIU/L

KETOSIS: NATURE'S BALANCE

Ketosis is a form of acidosis: a high saturation of acid in body tissues or fluids. It occurs when the energy your body needs to survive comes from fuel molecules called ketones and free fatty acids (FFA). The insulin: glucose link described above produces ketones, as stored fat is broken down as, by following a keto diet, there is no longer any new supply of glucose arriving into your body from the carbs you eat. The basic principle of the diet is that it is a low-carbohydrate, high-fat diet. So, ketosis is what causes weight loss and is what its dietary science is based on. Science tells us that ketosis produces 120 grams to 185 grams of ketones per day, compared to a ketoacidosis where over 400 grams per day are produced. The presence of ketones in your blood lowers its pH balance. An at home testing kit called 'Ketostix' can measure your blood ketone level and can be purchased easily online from Amazon. Your heart, brain, muscle tissue and kidneys use ketones for energy production. Science tells us that the human brain takes about two to three weeks to switch over to using ketones as energy to fuel itself, meaning it uses around 25 percent of glucose as fuel thereafter and it derives this from the glucose: glycogen balancing act described previously. A non-keto dieter's blood pH is around 7.4 and a pH of 7.2 is usual for someone in ketosis on a keto diet. Research in Sweden indicates that a LCHF / keto diet increases HDL levels without affecting LDL, assuming a daily carb intake of <20—25 grams per day as required for ketosis.

Carbohydrates are an obvious and delicious but deadly source of energy. Simple sugars from foods like bread, rice and candy are broken down quickly and easily, and will provide you with enough fuel to get through your day. A steady carb intake from breakfast to supper allows your body to function smoothly. But here's where we run into a problem: any excess simple sugars will be stored as fat to be burned later; for example, if you skip a meal. If you are consistently consuming more than your body needs to survive, this will most likely lead to weight gain, especially if you're not exercising. A bodily fat store is necessary in order to keep you going between meals, but in today's world of sedentary workdays and XL portion sizes, many of us keep a continuous store of fat will never burn, and consequently gain a significant amount of weight.

At times when you don't have a steady source of carbohydrates, your body has to draw fat from its stores to burn for energy. Quite simply, the burning of fat is ketosis, and the byproduct of this process are ketones. In this way, we can regard ketosis as the body's natural 'back-up plan', an alternative to burning carbs, in the interest of your survival. As you might expect, ketosis is an excellent way to lose weight because it means you're now burning fat instead of the daily carbs entering your system. Unfortunately, entering ketosis takes time, and any progress you have made towards reaching it is instantly negated as soon as you go back to eating high-carb foods which exceed your daily carb limit, as your body reverts to burning it for energy instead of your stored fat. Luckily, you can substitute carbs with healthy fats and some protein to trigger ketosis.

The maximum amount of carbs you can consume daily on a keto diet will of course vary from person to person. However, the threshold generally sits at less than 25 grams per day, before exiting ketosis. 15 grams is equal to an average meal. So, such a low carb budget must be obtained from healthy choices, in particular from vegetables. A basic keto meal combines proteins from naturally derived and grass-fed meat or fish with a large helping of non-starchy vegetables, like salad, zucchini or asparagus. Eating protein on a keto diet is essential too, so that your body does not break down stored protein inside your muscles and organs and, instead, derives it from the protein you eat, meaning those vital bodily parts remain unharmed.

Since your fat intake is largely unrestricted on a keto diet, healthy fats derived from olive oil and avocados can be eaten to compensate for the carb-rich vegetable oils, seeds and starches that will be missing from your diet, such as rice and potatoes. Maintaining ketosis is the key to forcing your body into a metabolic state. Starvation is not the objective here, but rather carb starvation. Your body's innate evolutionary ability to adapt to drastic changes in diet means that when you fill it with fats instead of carbs, you will start to burn ketones as for energy rather than glucose. Eventually, you will burn ketones at such a rate that you'll see the weight dropping off.

ACHIEVE KETOSIS!

Ever since the dawn of humanity in East Africa, the human diet has always been based on consuming three simple macronutrients: protein, fat and carbohydrate.

1. **Carbohydrate:** A food group comprised of sugars, such as glucose, derived from high-carb foods like starch and grains.
2. **Fat:** A food group used as energy by your body to build hormones and cells and is divided into three types: saturated, polyunsaturated and monounsaturated fats.
3. **Protein:** A nutrient formed of 22 amino acids which your body uses as energy to build muscle mass.

Entering ketosis requires that you keep your carb consumption between 5% to 10% of your daily calorific intake, fat between 60% to 75%, and protein between 15% to 30%. They are your keto macros. The term 'macro' is an abbreviation of the word 'macronutrient', which in turn refers to 'the big three': carbohydrates, proteins, and fats. Use an online macro calculator to calculate your optimal daily intake requirements. Fats cause a minute amount of glucose to be released when our bodies convert triglycerides; as a result, it is said that fats are 90% ketogenic and 10% anti-ketogenic. Proteins are roughly 45% ketogenic and 55% anti-ketogenic, as half of the proteins we consume are converted to glucose, which leads to a rise in blood insulin level. Carbs are 100% anti-ketogenic and are the main culprits in spiking our insulin and blood glucose levels. So, what does this mean? Simply put, carbs and protein are our main obstacles when trying to reach ketosis. It is, therefore, vital to understand the metabolic pathways through which they are converted into energy after we eat them. This proportion of macro nutrients allows your body to produce ketones as an energy source, which is what occurs when your body enters ketosis.

On an average balanced diet, carbs are processed by being turned into glucose (sugar) for energy. When ketosis is achieved, conversely, your body begins to use ketones, which are produced during the transfer of fat to energy. By maintaining ketosis, you transition into a metabolic state in which your body burns ketones. Ketosis happens naturally when your glucose levels are low. As we've already seen, it can be used to mitigate symptoms of epilepsy and can also be instrumental to weight loss, which can of course help boost your self-esteem and overall well-being. Not only that, but ketosis can help strengthen your body's resistance to insulin, meaning it is an effective treatment for diabetics. Let's go back to ketones for a moment. Ketones, or ketone bodies, are by-products of the breakdown of fat into energy. Their production works like this:

- When your glucose level is low, your glycogen levels are depleted.
- Your body must find alternative energy resource as fuel: fat
- Ketones, acetoacetate, acetone and β-hydroxybutyrate, are produced by your liver as fuel.
- Your body switches from being glucose fueled to fat fueled.
- When this happens over time, ketosis is achieved.

On the first day of ketosis, your glycogen level is depleted. Within three days, your insulin level is sustained, and your body burns fat as energy. Your body burns this fat by breaking it up into ketones, described above, and one glycerol molecule that makes new blood cells and bone marrow because their production cannot be fuelled by ketones. All other cell and tissue function relies on ketones. Achieve ketosis by:

- ✓ **Limiting carbohydrate:** Eat less than 25 grams of carbs per day.
- ✓ **Limiting protein:** Too much protein can reduce your blood ketone level (by gluconeogenesis) and therefore restrict your ability to enter ketosis. If you want to achieve a coveted lean body type, you want to eat about 0.6—0.8 grams of protein per pound consumed.
- ✓ **Eat healthy fats:** Though it might seem counterintuitive to weight loss, fat, especially healthy fat intake such as monosaturated and some polyunsaturated fats, is what the keto diet is based on as fat becomes your primary source of energy. Contrary to popular belief, starving yourself is not how a successful keto diet works. A successful keto diet depends on a careful balance of low carb and high fat foods.
- ✓ **Avoid unhealthy trans fats:** Processed foods such as takeaways, prepackaged foods and snacks contain processed and trans fats and sugars. Eating them causes your blood glucose levels to spike randomly and uncontrollably throughout the day, which negatively affects your ability to enter and maintain ketosis. Junk food such as sweet and savory snacks are the usual culprits that mess up any attempt to give the keto diet an honest and successful attempt, so be mindful of how much bad fats your food contains—remember to read the food labels.
- ✓ **Drink water:** Water contains electrolytes that help maintain normal bodily processes and function such as ketosis. You should drink enough to stay hydrated throughout the day, depending on your body and climate.
- ✓ **Exercise:** For decades, science has continually found exercise to have many health benefits for us humans, in addition to weight loss. Exercise burns calories (energy), meaning you deplete your daily calorific budget faster through doing more physical work, in addition to relying on ketosis to do the work for you. To get the most out of your keto diet, increase your current daily exercise routine by 20 or 30 minutes, even if it's just a leisurely walk. Every little helps towards regulating your blood sugar, remaining in ketosis and achieving weight loss As a general rule, I like to go for a quick 10 minute walk every day around my local park. As they say, exercise is great for releasing positive endorphins and is a great regulator of bodily health and mental wellbeing.

✓ **Consume supplements** – While this is not a necessity, supplements, such as Vitamin and Mineral supplements, have nutritional benefits. Be super careful, though, as many supplements, especially multivitamins, come loaded with sugar and harmful additives which can disrupt the chemical balance in your body, which is especially harmful to ketosis. As you know, ketosis is critical to the keto diet because it is the mechanism by which weight loss is achieved, so avoid upsetting this natural cycle by excluding artificial and manufactured products.

You might be wondering what kind of toll ketosis may exert on your body, especially if you're used to consuming higher amounts of carbs. Your body may have built up a stock of carbohydrate-active enzymes, and therefore might not be well-equipped to break down and store large volumes of fat, or to deal with a sudden shortage of glucose. As a result, your body will produce an entirely new supply of enzymes. After an adjustment period, your body will naturally begin to use your reserves of glucose, stored in your liver and muscles, for energy. This can lead to lethargy and sluggishness. Many people cite dizziness, headaches and irritability as early side effects of ketosis, particularly during the first seven days. This is due to the depletion of electrolytes from your system, which is, of course, another reason to drink plenty of water to replenish your sodium levels. As a matter of fact, since sodium helps retain water in the body, many dieticians recommend upping your salt intake significantly. However, science also tells us a LCHF level of ketosis of around 25 grams carbs per day results in excellent physical and mental wellbeing. Fortunately, your body has a safety mechanism if your ketone blood level drops beyond a critical level; it will produce insulin, as explained. Diabetics be warned, as your body doesn't have this mechanism and so always monitor your ketone level manually.

KETOACIDOSIS

It must be underlined that ketosis is different from ketoacidosis, which is a metabolic state to which sufferers of type 1 diabetes are particularly susceptible. Ketoacidosis occurs when dangerously high levels of ketones accumulate in your blood (between three and five times higher than those you get with ketosis). Ketosis and ketoacidosis are sometimes confused; the important distinction to make is that, while ketoacidosis can be life-threatening, ketosis is a natural bodily process that, when properly monitored, results in weight loss. Overall, science tells us that ketosis is an important mechanism for weight loss to occur on the keto diet, and without it, weight loss would be greatly reduced, and the diet would simply not work in the sense it does today.

SO...

Ketosis is a natural rejuvenating bodily state. It is state that our body enters to fuel itself; our body takes refuge in ketosis. Our body enters ketosis because it doesn't have enough carbohydrate from food to stay alive: a carb deficit. This is because, on a keto diet, we consume low-carb foods. Our body enters ketosis when we eat under 25 grams carbs per day and exits it when we eat over 50 grams of carbs per day. Think of ketosis as a cold shower for our body. When we are dirty, or fat, we turn on the water, ketosis and cleanse our body of years of accumulated and unwanted dirt and toxins: we lose weight. When we turn off the water, we exit ketosis and step out of the shower when we are clean, or at our desired weight.

FATS & OILS

THE GOOD & BAD

WHY are humans so afraid of fat? Science would suggest our fear of fat began in the 1970s decade with an American scientist called Ancel Keys. Since then, humans all over the world are making conscious and concerted efforts to eat less fat: global fat consumption has declined by over 10% since this time. Yet, rates of obesity, diabetes and cancer have all increased, especially in the West where efforts to reduce fat intake are most fierce. Fortunately, fat is key to a successful keto diet. However, the diet is only successful if you consume the right type of it. Unfortunately, there are good and bad fats, which can be confusing for beginners. So, let's cut through the confusion and discuss which fats you should eat. Fats divide into four groups:

1. **Saturated**
2. **Monounsaturated**
3. **Polyunsaturated**
4. **Trans**

Food often contains a mixture of each of those fats. Let's consider each type of fat more closely on a LCHF / keto diet.

SATURATED FAT

Saturated fat is key to human survival, but it is the fat science scrutinizes most. It is formed by membranes and phospholipids in cells of fatty acids found throughout the human body, especially the brain where over 70% of fat is saturated. Interestingly, fat is responsible for human emotions such as pleasure and is responsible for absorbing fat-soluble Vitamins A, D and E. Yet, saturated fat gets a bad rep in by science. Science has told us to avoid it, with research indicating that it causes a myriad of unwanted health issues such as obesity and diabetes. However, research by the Swedish council (SBU) found no strong correlation between consuming saturated fat and developing heart disease, for example. After all, this type of fat has been at the centre of the human diet since there were first humans: have humans evolved to accommodate it? Certain foods such as butter and palm oil contain medium-chain triglycerides (MCTs): your liver uses MCTs as energy. Science speaks of many more health benefits of saturated fat: (i) boosted immune system; (ii) improved HDL: LDL cholesterol ratio; (iii) improved bone density; (iv) increased testosterone and cortisol production. So, saturated fat is beneficial for weight loss on the keto diet. You can find saturated fat in the following foods:

Butter, cocoa butter, coconut oil, cream, eggs, alcohol, lard, palm oil, red meat, bacon, pork, milk, cooking oil, sugar products, dairy and processed foods...

MONOUNSATURATED FAT

Science tells us that monounsaturated fat is healthier than saturated fat. The health industry, for example, embraces it as a good fat and it is often found in fish and seed oils. These oils, however, are to be avoided on the keto diet. High heat is involved in their production and, as such, they are unstable at a molecular level, often associating with highly inflammatory trans fats. An example of this is the ratio of omega-6 to omega-3. Science suggests a link between high amounts of omega-6 and disease-causing inflammation. Some oils, such as extra virgin oil, olive oil and macadamia oils contain monounsaturated fatty acids (MUFAs) and are generally beneficial. They offer insulin resistance, lower blood pressure and a reduced heart disease risk. On balance, however, steering clear of oils derived from monounsaturated fat is recommend: the FDA prohibits them from baby food for retarding infant growth. I recommend reading Professor Mary Enig's research, *The Oiling of America*, to understand more about the dangerous effects of monounsaturated fats and oils on human health.

POLYUNSATURATED & TRANS FATS

Polyunsaturated fat is found in plant and animal foods, such as dairy, salmon, vegetable oils and nuts and seeds. Old cookery books commonly use animal fats found in nature, such as oil, lard, butter and bacon fat. Since the advancement of science and genetic engineering, oils are now derived from seeds. Have you seen an oily vegetable in nature? Of course not! Vegetable oils do not occur naturally; they are made from genetically modified seeds such as canola, corn, sunflower and cottonseed and contain long chains of polyunsaturated fatty acids (PUFAs). Those oils are cheap and easy to produce at a mass scale but are laced with dangerous health effects. As with monounsaturated fats, science criticizes the production process of genetically modified seeds. Over 70% of canola oil grown in the United States is genetically modified. PUFAs subjected to heat create uncharged molecules, or free radicals in the health industry, and cause inflammation and heart disease. So, if you must eat them, eat them cold, avoiding the lethal cooking process. Cold forms of those oils come in the form of Vitamin and Nutrient supplements but also superfoods such as salmon, flaxseed and sesame seeds and their consumption is encouraged. They contain heart-friendly fats such as omega 3 and omega 6. Science tells us that an ideal ratio of omega-3 and omega-6 is 1:1 but this is 1:30 in populations in the West. Striving to maintain this optimal ratio of omega-3 and omega-6 reduces the risk of heart disease, stroke, depression and ADHD. So, eating warm 'activated' polyunsaturated fat is discouraged, whereas eating cold 'dormant' polyunsaturated fat offers health benefits. To avoid polyunsaturated fats altogether, try finding foods produced wholly by nature, such as avocado, nuts and seeds, eggs, coconut oil and poultry.

Trans fats are the worst of the bunch! They include processed fats found in processed foods such as sweets, savory and snacks and are extremely damaging to your success on the keto diet. They contain hydrogenated and partially hydrogenated oils. Science indicates a relationship between those super long chain fats and increased risk of cancer, heart disease and inflammatory health, as they are more difficult for your liver to break down. But, as with the other fat types, while trans fats are decidedly unhealthily, there is one naturally occurring variety that is decidedly beneficial: vaccenic acid. Vaccenic acid is found across grass-fed meats and dairy products such as certain butters and yogurts. Ultimately, though, most processed foods like cookies, crackers, chips and a variety and fast foods have large quantities of trans fat and should be avoided on the keto diet.

WOMEN & WEIGHT LOSS

History tells us that women have struggled. Unfortunately, a LCHF diet such as the keto diet doesn't make women immune to struggling. There are several reasons why women aren't as fortunate as men when it comes to losing weight. The most important reason is fat and its relationship with their hormones. Men don't have hormones. Women do. This means that, while women suffer more intense emotional swings than men; they also store more weight too! They also metabolize fat differently than men and this, together with their tendency to eat more dairy foods such as creams and yogurts, makes weight loss extra challenging for them. So, as a woman, there is a way around this obstacle. Pay attention to thyroid health. Your thyroid controls your metabolism which, in turn, controls ketosis and your ability to lose weight. Finally, women have a self-sabotaging personality, so try not to treat yourself to a cheeky snack when you start seeing weight loss results.

IN SUMMARY...

GOOD FATS	BAD FATS
Coconut	Canola oil
Butter	Trans fats
Ghee	Processed fats
Olive oil	Butter
Avocado oil	Sunflower & flaxseed oils
Animal fats	Vegetable oil, heated
Naturally derived fats	Fish oil, heated
Pecan oil	Hydrogenated & partially hydrogenated oils

Fats are key to a successful keto diet. There four main types of fat, with each type doing and offering something a little different. So, it is important to know their differences. I can't stress enough the importance of consciously selecting which type of fat is best for you. Critically, though, is that saturated fats are not the boogeymen they've often been portrayed to be, but the best fats will always be those which are unprocessed. Processed and packaged foods are major stoppers to ketosis, weight loss and heart health. You should avoid them at all costs and choose healthier fats instead. Dieters must be cautious in their fat choices as each one offers both positive and negative health benefits. For this reason, I often refer to the keto diet as a low-carb healthy fat, as opposed to low-carb high fat, diet. For more information on choosing the right fats, feel free to do your own online research online. Sharing information over social media is a great way to stay in tip top shape as you show off your newly found body to the world.

KETO SIDE EFFECTS

A WORTHWHILE STRUGGLE...

THE transition to LCHF diet such as the keto diet is both physically and mentally taxing on your body. This transition from an unhealthy to healthy body state is not smooth and it is common to experience bumps along the road to a new you. The daily calorie budget promoted in this book of 1200 for men and 1000 for women is sharp; it is designed for quick and fast ketosis to achieve quick and fast weight loss. This means that you are likely to experience more side effects than you otherwise would following a keto diet based on a higher daily calorie budget. There are so many resources available, whether online, word of mouth or on the back of a food packet, that can overwhelm you. Those sources are sometimes conflicting, confusing you further. This is especially so when it comes to achieving real and effective ketosis, but also the various side effects your body may experience when transitioning to this healing state. For me, there is no shortcut! For others, the only way to figure out ketosis is to jump straight in and make the appropriate changes to your diet. Whichever type of person you are, you will inevitably experience negative, but temporary, side effects of ketosis. So, I recommend learning how to identify them at an early stage. They commonly manifest as visual symptoms, which confirm you are entering it. For example, you might like to try measuring your blood ketone levels with strip tests. So, most side effects of the diet are a direct result of ketosis. So, on a keto diet, people experience more side effects than on other diets. But the struggle is worthwhile, as millions of people have shown. The common side effects of the keto diet are:

Constipation: You may find it difficult to pass bodily fluids and suffer moments of constipation. This is normal and part of the adaptive transition to ketosis. You can mitigate it by drinking water and staying hydrated. You can also consume naturally derived supplements such as magnesium citrate from chia seeds. You can also mitigate constipation physically by doing exercise such as yoga and stretching that stimulates your gut in the morning and before bed.

Urination: Ketones can induce a diuretic response. The keto diet increases the volume of acetoacetate in your body, which is excreted in urine. As a result, you might find yourself making trips to the bathroom more often than normal. This is usually limited to the initial stages of ketosis, so at the start of the diet.

Thirst: You can attribute these side effects to the increased urination. To fight these symptoms, it's important to drink lots of water to replenish your electrolytes. This symptom can vary depending on your wider food choices; each food has different, conflicting, ingredients.

Bad breath: Acetone, one of our three ketone bodies, is excreted into the mouth during ketosis. Some people find this makes their breath smell like ripe fruit or nail polish remover, while other describe the smell as more akin to nail polish remover. Thankfully, this will go away with time, especially with good hygiene health.

Appetite: Once you're past the keto flu, you will find your energy is higher, your state of mind clearer and your hunger reduced. This is because your stomach has now shrunken to a smaller size as a consequence of ketosis, meaning you feel full up for longer on less food eaten.

Keto flu: Ketosis may cause flu-like symptoms. They may manifest as mild cramps, nausea, headaches and fatigue. They are temporary symptoms, lasting only a few days. Despite its name, keto flu (also known as the 'low-carb flu') has no relation to any kind of influenza. It is so-called because many newcomers to the keto diet experience several flu-like symptoms in the early stages of ketosis. Urination causes keto flu. Increased urination leads to a considerable loss of electrolytes and water in your body, disrupting its chemical balance. You can pre-emptively combat this problem by drinking a bouillon cube dissolved in water or take 1 gram of Vitamin C every few hours. Bone broth is also an excellent way of combating the cramps.

Withdrawal: Remember, your body is going through a major transition during ketosis! It has to adjust to a sharp drop in carb intake and create new enzymes in order to process increased amounts of fat. This is hard work for your body from an energy perspective, and you may feel lethargic as a result. To ease this, you should try decreasing your carb intake gradually and drink more water, which will replenish lost electrolytes and help maintain optimal bodily process and function. At the start of your transition to ketosis, you should eat fewer than 25 grams of carbs a day.

Fatigue: During the transition to ketosis, it is common to experience moments of fatigue. While a high blood ketone level can positively impact your physical wellbeing in several ways, they are also linked to increased tiredness and quicker exertion during exercise. If you experience prolonged and sustained moments of fatigue, you may not be eating enough protein; it is the nutrients derived from the protein which your body uses as energy.

'Brain fog': You may suffer from dizziness, or 'brain fog', on the keto diet, even after your transition to ketosis; thus, this symptom is not like the others because it can persist many weeks into the diet. It is caused by eating more low carb foods: carbs, specifically the glucose in them, controls your blood pressure. Your altered metabolism and hormonal state as a result of ketosis may cause decreased mental clarity or 'brain fog.' Other reasons include a magnesium or salt deficiency, which is why eating naturally derived supplements is a good option. This is a common side effect, which is why you should avoid going cold turkey and instead decrease your carb intake gradually and steadily in the first few weeks on the diet.

Lipids: The keto diet changes your blood readings. Your HDL and LDL blood readings will change during your transition to and out of ketosis. You should regularly get your bloods done to detect any potential problems with them. An important tenet of the keto diet is not only to up your healthy fat intake but also be mindful of which types of fats you eat. Saturated fats are known to increase cholesterol levels, for example. There is a lot of complexity surrounding fats on the keto diet. Please read the 'Fats & Oils' section of this book to learn more about the good and bad fat choices on the diet.

Micronutrient: The keto diet cuts out large amounts of protein and carbs. These 'banned' foods contain useful Vitamins and Minerals, whilst being unfriendly for ketosis. Low-carb foods promoted on the keto diet often lack important nutrients like magnesium, potassium and iron. Taking naturally derived supplements is an excellent way of compensating for this.

Ketoacidosis: If your diet is poorly planned, you may be at risk of developing ketoacidosis, which is characterized by extremely high ketone levels. This is especially harmful to sufferers of diabetes, so make sure you organize your diet to keep your ketone levels within a healthy range. Additionally, it is important to know how to recognize the signs. Science tells us that ketosis produces 120 grams to 185 grams of ketones per day, compared to a ketoacidosis where over 400 grams per day are produced A non-keto dieter's blood pH is around 7.4 and a pH of 7.2 is usual for someone in ketosis on a keto diet.

KETO BENEFITS

HEALTHY BODY!

ALL diets are met with criticism; the keto diet is no exception. Concerns are raised about the high fat intake that it promotes, as science tells us that fatty foods are known to raise cholesterol and cause heart disease. Yet, if healthy fats are chosen, the diet can reduce cholesterol. Success with the diet depends on the choices, patience, and discipline of the individual, not science. But what science does tells us is that the diet, if carefully planned and its ketosis principles respected, trumps all other diets. Weight loss is the main driver of going keto. This is a given. But the diet offers so many more health benefits. Some benefits are physical, such as weight loss, whereas others are mental and psychological. Let's not forget that your body, as a product of nature, is a network of both physical and mental processes; both must work optimally and together for you to feel and operate at your very best. When asking ourselves what benefits the diet offers, we must consider how the it works, fundamentally. Ketosis is the focus of the diet; it is the process which produces the most benefits, from weight loss to improving health and wellbeing. Ketosis is a metabolic state associated with numerous health benefits. The 'improve, protects and lowers' rule summarizes the main advantage of ketosis from a metabolic angle:

- ✓ Ketosis **improves** your body's ability to use stored fat as a source of energy.
- ✓ Ketosis **protects** your proteins, as your body uses ketones as sources of energy.
- ✓ Ketosis **lowers** blood insulin levels, which controls hormone balance.

How does this rule show to you? It is responsible for creating the visual changes and improvements you see happen to your body during ketosis as you transition through keto. So, let's consider more closely some of those visual cues of the benefits of the diet.

Maximum weight loss: The keto diet is built on weight loss through ketosis. This is a fact. Science has repeatedly shown the diet to be more effective than other diets for weight loss. The American Medical Association found the diet over 33 percent more effective for weight loss than 10 popular diets, including the Atkins diet. What is also true of following a keto diet is that, in addition to losing fat (specifically fat stored around our body), we lose water mass. Yes, our body contains a substantial amount of water: water contains electrolytes (think of these as like an energy lubricant) which help our cells function and keeps us alive. They also have a mass and add to our overall weight when we stand on a scale and weigh ourselves. But, by eating low carb food choices on a keto diet, you can reduce excess water that has built up and been stored around your body, especially inside your muscles. You might notice that, over time, your skin appears firmer and your face less bloated, simply due to less unwanted water stored inside your body. Interestingly, is that the process of ketosis reduces your blood insulin level which, in turn, flushes surplus sodium from your body, meaning you lose weight in this respect too. Despite popular debate, keto cannot spot reduce fat. Science tells us that the order in which you lose fat is down to your genetics, more so than your environment. So, by following a keto diet, you'll not only loss fat mass, but water mass too. Collectively, this means that you have the potential to lose a significant amount of overall body weight in a relatively short space of time.

Minimum triglycerides: There has been extensive research published on the link between triglycerides and illnesses such as heart disease. Science tells us that there is another relationship between carbs and triglycerides. What does this mean? It means that, by following a keto diet, you will eat low carb foods, and this will decrease your chance of developing heart disease, simply as a result of there being fewer triglycerides in your body.

Good cholesterol: The medical industry frequently tells us of the harms of cholesterol on your body. You may be under the impression that cholesterol is universally bad for you. What they don't often remind us of, however, is good cholesterol, especially its benefits. There is, in fact, a form of cholesterol that reduces the risk of heart disease: high-density lipoprotein or HDL. The increased consumption of healthy fats on the keto diet raises levels of HDL in your blood and helps to eradicate bad cholesterol (LDL). Please read the 'Hormone Link' section of this book, where the balance between HDL and LDL is discussed more closely.

Lower blood sugar: Science tells us that the function and purpose of our digestive system is to break down high-carb foods into simple sugars, which inevitably elevate our blood sugar level. Insulin is needed to combat these toxins. A high-carb diet, such as a generic unhealthy diet, maintained over many years can interfere with your body's ability to produce insulin, leading to type II diabetes. The ketogenic diet is advantageous in this regard, as it lowers your blood sugar and insulin levels significantly, if ketosis is followed correctly.

Suppressed appetite: All diets require that you reduce food consumption in one way or another. Inevitably, this leads people to make so many mistakes simply because they give in to their appetite and cravings. This failure is not inevitable on the keto diet. Why? As discussed in earlier sections, the beauty of a LCHF diet such as the keto diet is that it reduces your appetite, while other diets do not. By cutting carbs and substituting them with healthy fats and protein, you cut your daily calorific intake without going hungry.

Treat cancer: Science tells us that our body was designed by nature and to work best under a disciplined diet, such as the keto diet. Research out of Sweden indicates that a keto diet can regulate your body's metabolic function and that this regulation is linked to a reduced risk of developing cancers, especially stomach and liver. Why? The principle of the keto diet as a low carb diet means that the food you eat is low in carbs, which means that it is low in glucose (sugar) which, in turns, means that it is low in the energy those cancer cells need to grow and multiply. So, the keto diet can, in principle, stop cancer cells in their tracks by simply starving them of energy. Interesting, right?

Treat metabolic syndrome: Metabolic syndrome is the medical term for a combination of diabetes, high blood pressure (hypertension) and obesity. It puts you at greater risk of getting coronary heart disease, stroke and other conditions that affect the blood vessels. There are numerous symptoms, including obesity, low HDL, high triglyceride levels, high blood sugar levels and blood pressure (>140/90 mmHg). As the keto diet is designed for weight loss, it can target the obesity symptom and help mitigate the syndrome through weight loss, especially ketosis which will help with controlling the high blood sugar and cholesterol.

Therapy for brain disorders: In humans, our brain accounts for ~2 percent of our body weight, but it consumes ~20 percent of glucose-derived energy making it the main consumer of glucose. So, our liver is important because it derives glucose from protein instead of high carb foods which we exclude from our keto diet. Ketosis is important because it produces ketones which our brains use as fuel. As the history of the keto diet indicates, ketones can help treat seizures and epilepsy.

KETO SUCCESS

STAYING FOCUSED

FOLLOWING any diet isn't easy. The keto diet is one of the trickier diets in the dietary arena, largely due to its reliance on ketosis for weight loss. Ketosis has, for this reason, been explained in detail in this book, in order to help you avoid elementary mistakes and pitfalls on the keto diet. Still, you may still hit a brick wall. Personally, it took me three attempts to start the keto diet, successfully. By this I mean to master ketosis such that my body could easily move in and out of it quickly and safely—like dancing! Your weight loss efforts might not show, or you simply might have given up hope and confidence. This is  psychological doubt; it can be remedied. Thankfully, there a list of many steps to kickstart your confidence on the diet. Let's not doubt the fact that the diet doesn't come without its stumbling blocks. So, the essential tips and tricks below are designed to help keep you on track as you progress further down the ketogenic road.

Hydration: As discussed in previous sections, science continually stresses the importance of keeping yourself hydrated. Specifically, you should aim to drink water within the first hour after waking up in the morning, and another glass before you go to bed. This will help your body heal and rejuvenate whilst you sleep.

Practice intermittent fasting: To decide if the keto diet is right for you, you can try a method called intermitting fasting. This mimics ketosis and can be thought of as a primitive version of it. You should divide your week, defined as a period of 7 days, into fasting and un-fasting days. You then steadily reduce your carb intake in the days leading up to your fasting days. Fasting days should be divided into two phases:

1. **Building phase:** The period of time between your first and last meal.
2. **Cleaning phase:** The period of time between your last and first meal.

To start, try a cleaning phase of between 12 and 16 hours and a building phase of between 8 and 12 hours. As your body adjusts to the change, you will find yourself in a position to tackle a 4—6-hour building time and an 18-20-hour cleaning phase. Over time, you will notice weight loss, if followed correctly.

Exercise regularly: The benefit of exercise on human health was evident even before science became science; it is how life on Earth evolved, fundamentally. On the keto diet, rigorous exercise can help activate glucose molecules called GLUT-4 which are needed to convert glucose to fat. Additionally, it can double the amount of protein present in both the liver and the muscles, meaning you build muscle whilst burning fat.

Improve bowel movements: As outlined previously, constipation is a common symptom of following a keto diet. Thankfully, it can easily be combatted by consuming fermented foods like sauerkraut, coconut water and kimchi. You may also want to try naturally derived supplements like magnesium. Green tea, too, has been shown to add to the levels of calcium, magnesium and potassium in your body, all of which are useful in fighting constipation.

Limit protein consumption: Protein is integral to the keto diet but maintaining a proper balance is a must. If you eat too many protein-rich foods, you will end up converting the amino acids into glucose (through a process called gluconeogenesis). In the initial stages of your keto diet, vary the amounts of protein you consume to get a feel of how much is too much for your dietary needs.

Take MCT oil: As discussed in the 'Keto Diet History' section, MCT oil is principal to a modern keto diet. High-quality MCTs are extremely effective in replenishing energy levels which you deplete throughout the day. MCT oil can be used for cooking too, as well as added to beverages like coffee, tea, smoothies and protein shakes.

Period changes: Are you female? If so, ketosis affects your metabolism which, in turn, affects the timing and frequency of your periods. You can mitigate this by eating more fat, which will also make you more fertile, which is especially useful if you are planning for a child.

Minimize stress: Stress is a major factor that wanes your energy level. Constant stress, especially mental, may serve as a threat to ketosis. If you find yourself especially prone to stress, it may be wise to consult your physician before starting keto and get yourself in a better psychological position first.

Improve sleep: Sleep is essential for managing stress, among other things. Make sure your bedroom is conducive to a good night's rest. This means sleeping in a comfortable bed, in a darkened room no warmer than 70 degrees, as higher temperatures can affect your metabolism and ketosis. Science suggests that most adults function best on 7 to 9 hours of sleep every night, though a particularly stressful lifestyle may require even longer.

Eat ghee: Ghee works well as a butter substitute, as it can be used in all the same way in recipes and is considerably healthier. Try frying meat or vegetables in it for a high-fat, healthy meal, remembering to avoid vegetable oils.

Consume omega-3: If you find it hard to integrate omega-3-rich foods into your diet, you might consider taking supplements. You should make sure your omega-3 intake matches your Omega-6s. Omega-3 is an extremely beneficial fat, which is crucial to the keto diet, but only if it is consumed cold, as discussed in the 'hot Vs cold' fats section.

Avoid alcohol: It may be hard to give up alcohol. Science has continually made well-attested evidence that alcohol impedes ketosis and weight loss on the keto diet. Stay focused on your goals and order a glass of tonic water at the bar instead. Lemon water is a tasty and refreshing alternative too and has the added benefit of balancing your blood pH level.

Buy a food scale: Recipes, especially those on the keto diet, require exact ingredients. Food scales can help you bake with accuracy and save money; they are a great utensil to keep handy in your kitchen. They are indispensable in tracking your carbs and overall caloric intake. Invest in your success and get a high-quality, durable scale with a conversion button, automatic shutdown, tare function, and a removable plate.

Go international keto: Expand your culinary horizon and look towards International ketogenic approved foods. Shirataki noodles are made from yams and make a great low-carb alternative to pasta. You can buy them online from Amazon or even your local food store. Spaghetti squash is a new and iconic food to the keto diet that can be cut into the shape of noodles with the aid of a spiralizer or a fork. It tastes great and amounts to less than half the carbs and calories of conventional noodles. Shredded cauliflower is also another alterative and mimics the texture and neutral taste of white or brown rice. International cuisine offers many choices for the keto diet beyond the Western menu and is a great way to bridge out of the traditional food choices available on the keto diet. Be adventurous!

MEAL PLAN

30-DAYS OF KETO

ALL diets require a meal plan. Without one, you wouldn't lose weight effectively and we would spend a lot more of our time deciding on which foods to eat, which isn't ideal in our fast-paced daily life. A meal plan is essential for the keto diet. Ketosis requires disciplined eating to work, otherwise your weight loss wouldn't be consistent. Meal plans are an effective dietary tool because they allow you to plan your meals in advance. From this, meal prepping, that is the boxing and preparing of food in plastic containers, comes into play. But this involves buying a lot of food in advance from the grocery store, which is often tricky if you are a new dieter.

The meal plan in this book covers a 30-day period and is designed for beginners to the diet. It is an ideal and time efficient way to start the keto diet as a beginner, despite what other information and dieters may decide to promote. This is because it provides beginners with just the right balance of choice and freedom in their meals, whilst limiting them to the standard three meals per day: breakfast, lunch and dinner. These three meals make up your daily meal plan. Your task, as a meal planner, is to decide on which keto friendly meals you fill into those daily meal slots. I have done this work for you. In general:

- ✓ Keto meal plans start with a daily calorie budget: 1200 for males and 1000 for females.
- ✓ This is the calorie budget used in this book because it is designed to kickstart ketosis quickly.
- ✓ You decide which keto diet you follow. In this case, we chose a standard SKD plan that includes a macronutrient ratio of 75% fat, 20% protein and 5% carbs.
- ✓ You allocate this macro ratio to your calorie budget by selecting appropriate meals.
- ✓ Eliminate meals which include a high percentage of bad fats.
- ✓ The keto diet is not so reliant on proteins, so be careful not to over consume protein as too doing so leads to gluconeogenesis and disrupt ketosis.

The take home message is that calories, carbs and fats are the three most important macros to consider when inventing your meal plan. A daily plan can easily be turned into a weekly, monthly and yearly plan, simply by doing your own research. The plan below considers ketosis over time. If you look at the total calorie counts for each week, you may notice that they decrease over time. This is to allow you to safely kickstart ketosis, as a beginner to the diet. So, your chances of suffering keto side effects are greatly reduced. If you want to kickstart ketosis quickly, which I do not recommend, your week 1 calorie counts will be lower, as will your carbs too. In time, you will build up an effective meal plan that suits your tastes and budget, whilst complying with keto dietary rules and principles surrounding ketosis. To keep things as simple as possible, this meal plan is designed for one person. If you would like to use it for multiple people, simply multiply the ingredient quantities by the total number of people. Be flexible! Feel free to replace any of the recipes or ingredients with your personal choices and adjust the ingredients to fit your macros and eating habits. If you follow a very strict keto diet, make sure to personalize this plan, perhaps by including desserts and snacks too. The possibilities are infinite.

WEEK 1

DAY	BREAKFAST	LUNCH	DINNER	CALORIES	FAT	PROTEIN	CARBS
MONDAY	Cristy's Pancakes	Money Salad	Grilled Ham & Cheese	1310	106	83	4
TUESDAY	Breakfast Tea	Jarlsberg Lunch Omelet	Prosciutto Spinach Salad	834	67	47.5	5.5
WEDNESDAY	Sausage Quiche	Mu Shu Lunch Pork	Beef Casserole	1160	59	60	24
THURSDAY	Breakfast Sausage Casserole	Fiery Jalapeno Poppers	Easy Zoodles & Turkey Balls	1127	51	61	16
FRIDAY	Scrambled Mug Eggs	Bacon & Chicken Patties	Lasagna Spaghetti Squash	1170	83	74	10
SATURDAY	Banana Chia Seed Pudding	Rice Chicken Curry	Blue Cheese Chicken Wedges	774	52	36	19
SUNDAY	Strawberry Rhubarb Parfait	'I Love Bacon'	'Oh so good' Salad	947	93	39	11
WEEKLY TOTAL				6012	405	318	86

WEEK 2

DAY	BREAKFAST	LUNCH	DINNER	CALORIES	FAT	PROTEIN	CARBS
MONDAY	Avocado Toast	Duck Fat Ribeye	Stuffed Chicken Roles	1150	87	85	7
TUESDAY	Rubarb Parfait	Jarlsberg Lunch Omelet	Chicken in a Blanket	1354	111	57	11
WEDNESDAY	Sausage Egg Muffins	Dijon Halibut Steak	Riced Cauliflower & Curry Chicken	1760	100	99	16
THURSDAY	Breakfast Sausage Casserole	Roast Beef Lettuce Wraps	Mashed Garlic Turnips	900	68	47	15
FRIDAY	Salmon Omelet	Bacon & Chicken Patties	Chicken Tenders	1220	82	93	7.7
SATURDAY	Banana Chia Seed Pudding	Cheddar Bacon Burst	Fat Bombs	845	75	46	9
SUNDAY	Spinach Eggs & Cheese	Hamburger Patties	Nearly Pizza	1108	86	98	14
WEEKLY TOTAL				7187	522	440	73

WEEK 3

DAY	BREAKFAST	LUNCH	DINNER	CALORIES	FAT	PROTEIN	CARBS
MONDAY	Keto Pancakes	Lemon Dill Trout	Gluten Free Gratin	895	59	70	7
TUESDAY	Sausage Casserole	Jarlsberg Omelet	Prosciutto Salad	1014	80	58.5	5.5
WEDNESDAY	Sausage Egg Muffins	Easy Slider	Sausage Balls	1289	104	75	15
THURSDAY	Bacon Cups	'I Love Bacon'	Turkey Avocado Rolls	743	62	58	9
FRIDAY	Scotch Eggs	Cast Iron Chicken	Lasagne Spaghetti Squash	1184	88	75	9
SATURDAY	Fried Eggs	Bacon Chops	Bacon Scallops	939	78	52	13
SUNDAY	Hash Browns	'No Potato' Shepherd's Pie	Buffalo Chicken Salad	1010	46	36	23
			WEEKLY TOTALS	6179	458	355	75

WEEK 4

DAY	BREAKFAST	LUNCH	DINNER	CALORIES	FAT	PROTEIN	CARBS
MONDAY	Sausage Casserole	Bacon Butternut Squash	Browned Butter Asparagus	940	76	42.6	22
TUESDAY	Avocado Toast	Fiery Poppers	Brussels Sprouts & Bacon	820	32	42	15
WEDNESDAY	Fried Eggs	Turkey Roll Up	Mexican Taco Casserole	943	37.3	89	10.5
THURSDAY	Chocolate Waffles	Sweet Savory Chicken	Hamburger Patties	963	50.5	95.1	11.2
FRIDAY	Egg Crepes	Lemon Pepper Beans	Thai Curry	794	27.8	61.1	18.9
SATURDAY	Ham & Cheese Pockets	Cumin Spiced Beef Wraps	Bacon Scallops	910	67	104	11.8
SUNDAY	Clementine & Pistachio	Mahi Mahi Stew	Med. Turkey Cutlets	847	54	55.4	22
			WEEKLY TOTALS	5277	269	447	89

AFFORDABLE KETO

SHOPPING LISTS

SHOPPING on a keto diet should be fun and affordable! That's why there's four weekly shopping lists included in this section. They are designed to complement the weekly meal plans introduced in the previous section. Each list has all the food you need for your weekly meal plan. You can print them out and photograph them using your phone to take with you to the grocery store. Yes, it's time to go shopping! Take them to your grocery store and buy exactly what you need, nothing less or more. You'll know exactly the ingredients you need to buy, meaning you can plan your shopping budget in advance and save time and money. Get cooking those quick, tasty and affordable meals on a budget in no time at all.

FOODS TO AVOID

Everyone likes a quick snack! But this doesn't mean we should be clumsy in our eating habits. Committing to a keto diet requires discipline, especially when it comes to the fats and oil you eat on it. Some foods you should avoid at all costs because of their health implications. They include:

- ✓ Grains, in all forms. This means no rice, corn, oats, wheat, barley, pasta, bread, crackers and so forth.
- ✓ Factory-farmed fish and pork. Organic and local is always better quality.
- ✓ Processed foods, which are often high in sugar.
- ✓ Artificial sweeteners.
- ✓ Refined fats and oils, such as canola oil and soybean oil.
- ✓ Foods that claim to be "low-carb" or "zero-carb" – these labels are often deceptive.
- ✓ Milk, as it is high in carbs.
- ✓ Alcoholic and sweet beverages as they are often loaded with artificial sugars.

Cutting those foods from your diet will maintain ketosis and your weight loss efforts. Remember, snacking is a slippery slope, as one small snack often leads to larger one, and before you know it, your diet is ruined, and you find yourself back at where you started again. I like to weigh myself naked (clothes add to my weight unnecessary) and keep looking at myself in the mirror. A quick glance fills me with confidence to start my day with a smile!

SHOPPING TIPS

- Make sure you have your shopping lists before leaving the house!
- Focus on the fresh and natural food sections; avoid the junk food aisles.
- Be cautious of food with fancy packaging and slogans; it likely has a ton of sugar.
- Be mindful of food with a long list of ingredients; it may contain artificial substances that disrupt ketosis.
- Buy fresh, organic and pasture fed meat from the Deli counter.
- Scrutinize foods claiming to offer a health benefit such as weight loss and improved X and Y effects.

WEEK 1 -

30 eggs
40 slices bacon
1 cup almond meal
1 cup hazelnut meal
2 bananas
2 tea bags
2 tbsp. ghee
5 cups heavy cream
5 cups cheddar cheese
3 cups mozzarella cheese
1 cup parmesan cheese
3 tsp. blue cheese
1 oz. Jarlsberg cheese
30 oz. ricotta cheese
1 oz. cream cheese
1 tbsp. coconut oil
2 heads cauliflower (around 4 lb.)
1 ½ tbsp. vanilla extract
1 cup coconut milk
8.5 oz. plain yogurt
2 tbsp. butter
3 lb. pork sausage
1 pack buffalo sauce
½ tsp. cinnamon

¼ cup chia seeds
2 cups raw almond flakes
2 cups coconut flakes
1 tsp. low-carb strawberry &
rhubarb jam (4.25 oz.)
1 cup raw unsalted cashews
1 cup 90% dark chocolate
shavings
1 cup mushrooms
3 onions
3 oz. sliced ham
2 cups coleslaw mix
1 lb. roast pork
2 tbsp. hoisin sauce
2 tbsp. soy sauce
2 jalapeno peppers
½ tsp. Mrs. Dash Table Blend
1 ½ oz. chicken breast
5 tbsp. coconut flour
3 lb. chicken
(6 breasts)
1 packet curry paste
12 oz. steak
1 tbsp. butter

½ cup almond flour
1 tsp. baking powder
1 cup baby spinach
⅓ lb. prosciutto
½ cantaloupe
1 avocado
1 red onion
1 cup unsalted walnuts
1 ½ lb. ground beef
½ bag coleslaw mix
1 ½ cups tomato sauce
1 tbsp. lemon juice
1 zucchini
1 can vodka pasta sauce
6 meatballs
40 oz. Rao's Marinara sauce
44b oz. spaghetti squash
1 cup brussels sprouts
½ tsp. apple cider vinegar
1 tsp. grapeseed oil
1 packet KetogenX Vanilla
Skillet, ice cream maker, muffin
pan & Utensils
Salt & Pepper

WEEK 2 -

26 eggs
8.5 oz. plain yoghurt
1 tbsp. hazelnut meal
2 tbsp. toasted almond flakes
1 cup toasted coconut flakes
2 tbsp. low-carb strawberry and
rhubarb jam (4.25 oz.)
1 smoked salmon
1 banana
½ tsp. cinnamon
1 tsp. vanilla extract
¼ cup chia seeds
3-4 oz. spinach
16-oz. ribeye steak (1 - 1 ¼ inch
thick)
1 tbsp. duck fat (or other high smoke
point oil like peanut oil)
½ tsp. thyme
1 oz. slices ham
1 6-oz. fresh or thawed halibut steak
1 tbsp. lemon juice
½ tbsp. Dijon mustard
1 tsp. fresh basil
8 large iceberg lettuce leaves

8 oz. (8 slices) rare roast beef
½ cup homemade mayonnaise
1 cup baby spinach
5 tbsp. keto coconut flour
4-5 cups raw spinach
1-2 tbsp. Tones' Southwest Chipotle
Seasoning
2 tsp. Mrs. Dash Table Seasoning
1 lb. ground beef (or ½ lb. beef, ½ lb.
pork)
1 tbsp. minced garlic (or paste)
3 jalapeno peppers
1 packet curry paste
2 cloves garlic
1 4-oz. bag spicy pork
rinds/chicharrons
1 tsp. vanilla extract (gluten free)
½ tsp. nutmeg
8 large portobello mushrooms
2 tsp. olive oil
1 cup marinara sauce
10 slices pepperoni
4 cups heavy cream
50 slices bacon

2 onions
10 oz. pork sausage
2 cups provolone cheese
1 cup parmesan cheese
2 cups cheddar cheese
1 oz. Jarlsberg cheese
1 ½ cups mozzarella cheese
15 oz. cream cheese
2 heads cauliflower (1 kg)
5 tbsp. butter
3 tbsp. ghee (can substitute with
butter)
1 cup coconut butter
20 chicken breasts
3 cups coconut milk
Salt, pepper, garlic powder or other
seasonings
1 pack KetogenX Vanilla
Skillet, ice cream maker, muffin pan
Mixing bowl
Kitchen utensils

WEEK 3 -

32 eggs
1 tbsp. almond or hazelnut meal
2 heads cauliflower
2 lb. pan-dressed trout (or other small fish), fresh or frozen
2 tbsp. dill weed
2 tbsp. lemon juice
2 mushrooms
2 ½ lb. ground beef
Worcestershire sauce
1 oz. ranch dressing
4 onions
8 oz. low-carb mushroom sauce
¼ cup ketchup
1 lb. frozen mixed vegetables
1 lb. low carb bake mix or equivalent
1 cup baby spinach
⅓ lb. prosciutto
½ cantaloupe

1 avocado
¼ cup red onions
1 pack raw, unsalted walnuts
10 cubes cheddar (optional)
12 slices (12 oz.) turkey breast
2 cups baby spinach
1 avocado
1 cup mayonnaise
1 large jar (40 oz.) Rao's Marinara sauce
1 large spaghetti squash, cooked (44 oz.)
12 scallops
16 toothpicks
½ tbsp. olive oil
3 cups salad of your choosing
1 jar buffalo wing sauce of your choosing
25 slices mozzarella cheese
2 cups cheddar cheese

4 tsp. parmesan cheese
5 slices pepper jack cheese
1 oz. Jarlsberg or Swiss cheese
30 oz. ricotta cheese
12 slices Swiss cheese
67 slices bacon
1 cup butter
4 cups heavy cream
5 cups pork sausage
5 slices ham
2 slices tomato
5 chicken breasts
12 oz. steak
1 scoop of KetogenX Vanilla
Garlic, salt, pepper, onion powder to taste
Skillet & bowl
Kitchen utensils

WEEK 4 -

17 eggs
1 head cauliflower
1 lb. pork sausage
5 cups heavy cream
8 tbsp. sunflower oil
2 avocados
5 slices cauliflower bread
2 scoops vanilla protein powder
50 grams 90% chocolate chips
½ cup alfalfa sprouts
5 slices turkey breast
1 cup mozzarella cheese
2 tbsp. flax meal
3 oz. provolone cheese
3 oz. slices ham
2 tsp. pistachios
¾ cup ricotta
5 strawberries
2 segmented clementine
½ lb. butternut squash
2 jalapeno peppers
½ tsp. Mrs. Dash Table Blend

2 carrot sticks
3 tsp. mustard
1 tsp. brown sugar
½ tsp. onion powder
¾ lb. skinless chicken breast
1 tbsp. red pepper flakes
½ lb. boiled green beans
1 garlic clove
½ tsp. lemon pepper seasoning
4 lbs. ground beef
1½ tbsp. coconut oil
1 tsp. cumin
4 boiled cabbage leaves
10 oz. butter
¾ lb. cubed Mahi Mahi fillets
1 onion
¾ cup homemade fish broth
¼ cup sour cream
12 oz. green asparagus
5 oz. parmesan cheese
5 oz. brussels sprouts
½ tsp. dried rosemary

5 ⅓ cups cheddar cheese
⅓ cup low carb salsa
⅓ cup cottage cheese
¾ tbsp. taco seasoning
1½ oz. crumbled feta cheese
½ cup canned coconut milk
½ lb. pork tenderloin
1 tbsp. Thai curry paste
12 scallops
30 bacon slices
12 toothpicks
4 ½ tbsp. olive oil
¼ cup coconut flour
½ tsp. Greek seasoning
½ tsp. turmeric powder
Salt, Pepper
Skillet
Bowl
food blender
Kitchen utensils

CONVERSIONS

SPOONS & CUPS

TSP	TBSP	FL OZ	CUP	PINT	QUART	GALLON
3	1	1/2	1/16	1/32	–	–
6	2	1	1/8	1/16	1/32	–
12	4	2	1/4	1/8	1/16	–
18	6	3	3/8	–	–	–
24	8	4	1/2	1/4	1/8	1/32
36	12	6	3/4	–	–	–
48	16	8	1	1/2	1/4	1/16
96	32	16	2	1	1/2	1/8
–	64	32	4	2	1	1/4
–	256	128	16	8	4	1

MILLILITERS

TSP	ML
1/2	2.5
1	5

TBSP	ML
1	15

OZ	ML
2	60
4	115
6	150
8	230
10	285
12	340

CUP	ML
1/4	60
1/2	120
2/3	160
3/4	180
1	240

GRAMS

OZ	G	LB
2	58	–
4	114	–
6	170	–
8	226	1/2
12	340	–
16	454	1

KETO
~ RECIPES ~

"The keto diet has been around for decades, but the modern keto diet is a new 21ˢᵗ century invention."

KETO PANCAKES

Prep & Cook Time: 20 minutes | Servings: 4
260 cal., 22g fat, 8g protein & 4g carbs.

INGREDIENTS

5 large eggs
⅓ cup of unsweetened almond milk
1 tsp. of baking power
1 cup of almond flour
¼ cup of coconut flour

INSTRUCTIONS

1. In a large bowl, whisk all the ingredients together until a smooth mixture is formed. This is your batter for making your pancakes. The batter should take a consistency just right to pour into a pan to form a pancake. If it is too thick, add some almond milk until a typical pancake batter is formed. Be careful not to add too much milk, or your pancakes will turn out like scrambled eggs!
2. Grease a medium sized pan with avocado oil. This is a butter substitute and is necessary to prevent your batter sticking to the pan and burning.
3. Preheat the pan at 375°F for around 1-2 minutes.
4. Now, carefully pour the pancake batter into the hot pan to form pancake shapes.
5. Fry for 1-2 minutes until one side starts to bubble and is golden brown.
6. Now, flip and cook the other side for another 1-2 minutes, until browned. If you are an adventurous cook, you can put on your chef hat and flip the pancakes in the air as high as you can. Be careful not to hit the ceiling though!
7. Place a sheet of parchment paper onto a plate. Pencil your name on it!
8. Place the pancakes onto the paper on the plate. Repeat until the pancake mix is all gone...
9. Serve with whatever drink takes your fancy. I like coffee!

- -

BREAKFAST SANDWICH

Prep & Cook Time: 10 minutes | Servings: 2.
600 cal., 50g fat, 12g protein & 7g carbs.

INGREDIENTS

2 oz./60g cheddar cheese
1 oz./30g ham slices
2 tbsp. butter
4 eggs

INSTRUCTIONS

1. Fry all the eggs in a skillet on medium heat. Sprinkle the pepper and salt on top.
2. Place an egg down as the sandwich base. Top with the ham and cheese and a drop or two of Tabasco sauce.
3. Place the other egg on top and serve onto plates.
4. Enjoy.

- -

EGG MUFFINS

Prep & Cook Time: 30 minutes | Servings: 6
190 cal., 15g fat, 7g protein & 4g carbs.

INGREDIENTS

1 tbsp. green pesto
3 oz./75g cheddar cheese
5 oz./150g bacon slices, cooked

1 scallion, chopped
6 eggs

INSTRUCTIONS

1. Preheat your oven to 350°F/175°C.
2. Place liners in a regular cupcake tin. This will help with easy removal and storage.
3. Beat the eggs with the pepper, salt and pesto. Mix in the cheese.
4. Pour the egg mixture into the cupcake tin and top with the bacon and chopped scallion.
5. Cook for 15-20 minutes, or until the egg is set.
6. Serve onto plates!

- -

BACON & EGGS

Prep & Cook Time: 5 minutes | Servings: 4
180 cal., 7g fat, 14g protein & 5g carbs.

INGREDIENTS

Pinch parsley, chopped
1 tomato
⅓ oz./150g bacon slices
8 eggs

INSTRUCTIONS

1. Fry up the bacon in a skillet on a medium heat and put it to the side.
2. Scramble the eggs in the bacon grease with some pepper and salt. If desired, scramble in some cherry tomatoes.
3. Sprinkle with some parsley and enjoy.

- -

EGGS ON THE GO

Prep & Cook Time: 10 minutes | Servings: 6
175 cal., 6g fat, 8g protein & 1g carbs.

INGREDIENTS

2 oz./50g bacon slices, cooked
Pepper & Salt
6 eggs

INSTRUCTIONS

1. Preheat your oven to 400°F/200°C.
2. Place liners in a regular cupcake tin. This will help with easy removal and storage.
3. Crack an egg into each of the cups and sprinkle some bacon onto each of them. Season with some pepper and salt.
4. Bake for 15 minutes, or until the eggs are set.
5. Enjoy.

- -

CREAM CHEESE PANCAKES

Prep & Cook Time: 10 minutes | Servings: 1
340 cal., 30g fat, 7g protein & 3g carbs.

INGREDIENTS

2 oz. cream cheese
2 eggs
½ tsp. cinnamon
1 tbsp. coconut flour
½ to 1 packet Stevia

INSTRUCTIONS

1. In a bowl, mix together all the ingredients until smooth.
2. Heat up a non-stick pan or skillet with butter or coconut oil on medium-high.

3. Prepare the pancake mix as you would normal pancakes.
4. Pour into a skillet and cook it on one side and then flip to cook the other side!
5. Top with some butter and/or sugar-free syrup.
6. Serve onto plates and enjoy.

BREAKFAST MIX
Prep & Cook Time: 15 minutes | Servings: 1
150 cal., 9g fat, 8g protein & 4g carbs.

INGREDIENTS
5 tbsp. coconut flakes, unsweetened
7 tbsp. hemp seeds
5 tbsp. flaxseed, ground
2 tbsp. sesame, ground
2 tbsp. cocoa, dark, unsweetened
INSTRUCTIONS
1. Grind the flaxseed and the sesame. Make sure you only grind the sesame seeds for a very short period.
2. Mix all ingredients in a jar and shake it well.
3. Keep refrigerated until ready to eat.
4. Serve softened with black coffee or even with still water and add coconut oil if you want to increase the fat content. It also blends well with cream or with mascarpone cheese.

BREAKFAST MUFFINS
Prep & Cook Time: 30 minutes | Servings: 1
150 cal.,11g fat, 7g protein & 12g carbs.

INGREDIENTS
1 egg
¼ cup heavy cream
1 slice cooked bacon (cured, pan-fried, cooked)
1 oz. cheddar cheese
Salt and black pepper (to taste)
INSTRUCTIONS
1. Preheat your oven to 350°F/175°C.
2. In a bowl, mix the eggs with the cream, salt and pepper.
3. Spread into muffin tins and fill the cups half full.
4. Place 1 slice of bacon into each muffin hole and half ounce of cheese on top of each muffin.
5. Bake for around 15-20 minutes or until slightly browned.
6. Add another ½ oz. of cheese onto each muffin and broil until the cheese is slightly browned.
7. Serve!

EGG PORRIDGE
Prep & Cook Time: 15 minutes | Servings: 2
604 cal., 45g fat, 8g protein & 3g carbs.

INGREDIENTS
2 eggs
⅓ cup heavy cream
2 tbsp. Stevia
2 tbsp. butter
Pinch organic cinnamon to taste
INSTRUCTIONS
1. In a bowl add the eggs, cream and sweetener, and mix together.

2. Melt the butter in a saucepan over a medium heat. Lower the heat once the butter is melted.
3. Combine together with the egg and cream mixture.
4. While Cooking, mix until it thickens and curdles.
5. When you see the first signs of curdling, remove the saucepan immediately from the heat.
6. Pour the porridge into a bowl. Sprinkle cinnamon on top and serve!

EGGS FLORENTINE
Prep & Cook Time: 20 minutes | Servings: 2
180 cal., 10g fat, 7g protein & 5g carbs.

INGREDIENTS
1 cup spinach leaves, washed
2 tbsp. parmesan cheese, grated
Sea salt & pepper
1 tbsp. white vinegar
2 eggs
INSTRUCTIONS
1. Cook the spinach in the microwave on a medium setting, or steam, until wilted.
2. Sprinkle with parmesan cheese and seasoning.
3. Slice into bite-size pieces and place on a plate.
4. Simmer a pan of water on medium heat and add the vinegar. Stir quickly with a spoon.
5. Break an egg into the center. Turn off the heat and cover until set.
6. Repeat with the second egg.
7. Place the eggs on top of the spinach and serve onto plates.
8. Enjoy!

SPANISH OMELET
Prep & Cook Time: 15 minutes | Servings: 3
160 cal., 15g fat, 7g protein & 4g carbs.

INGREDIENTS
3 eggs
Pinch black pepper
½ cup finely chopped vegetables of your choosing.
INSTRUCTIONS
1. In a skillet on high heat, stir-fry the vegetables in extra virgin olive oil until lightly crisp.
2. Cook the eggs with one tbsp. of water and a pinch of pepper.
3. When almost cooked, top with the vegetables and flip to cook briefly.
4. Serve!

CRISTY'S PANCAKES
Prep & Cook Time: 10 minutes | Servings: 1
300 cal., 30g fat, 8g protein & 2 carbs.

INGREDIENTS
1 scoop KetogenX Vanilla
1 tbsp. almond or hazelnut meal
2 tbsp. water
1 egg
INSTRUCTIONS
1. Add the ingredients together in a bowl and mix together to form the mixture.

2. Pour the mixture into a greased skillet to form circle sized pancakes.
3. Fry on a medium heat for approximately 2 to 3 minutes on each side. (Watch carefully as it may stick and burn quickly).
4. Serve buttered onto plates with a handful of mixed berries.

BREAKFAST TEA
Prep & Cook Time: 5 minutes | Servings: 1
110 cal., 12g fat, 1g protein & 1g carbs.

INGREDIENTS
16 oz. water
2 tea bags
1 tbsp. ghee
1 tbsp. coconut oil
½ tsp. vanilla extract
INSTRUCTIONS
1. Make the tea and put it aside.
2. In a skillet on a low heat, melt the ghee.
3. Add the coconut oil and vanilla to the melted ghee. Turn off the heat and stir until warm.
4. Pour the tea from a cup into a Nutribullet cup.
5. Screw on the lid and blend thoroughly.
6. Pour into cups and drink!

SAUSAGE QUICHE
Prep & Cook Time: 35 minutes | Servings: 6
335 cal., 30g fat, 11g protein & 2g carbs.

INGREDIENTS
12 large eggs
1 cup heavy cream
1 tsp. black pepper
12 oz. pork sausage
2 cups cheddar cheese, shredded
INSTRUCTIONS
1. Preheat your oven to 375°F/190°C.
2. In a large bowl, whisk the eggs, heavy cream, sausage and pepper together.
3. Add the breakfast sausage and cheddar cheese.
4. Pour the mixture into a greased casserole dish.
5. Bake for 25 minutes in the oven.
6. Cut into 12 squares and serve hot.

BREAKFAST SAUSAGE CASSEROLE
Prep & Cook Time: 50 minutes | Servings: 4
290 cal., 25g fat, 12g protein & 1g carbs.

INGREDIENTS
8 eggs, beaten
1 head cauliflower, chopped
1 lb. pork sausage, cooked & crumbled
2 cups heavy cream
1 cup cheddar cheese, grated
INSTRUCTIONS
1. Preheat your oven to 375°F/190°C and cook the sausage as usual.
2. In a large bowl, mix the cooked sausage, heavy whipping cream, chopped cauliflower, cheese and eggs.
3. Pour into a greased casserole dish.

4. Cook for 45 minutes at 350°F/175°C, or until firm.
5. Top with cheese and serve.
6. Enjoy!

SCRAMBLED MUG EGGS
Prep & Cook Time: 5 minutes | Servings: 1
330 cal., 30g fat, 12g protein & 1g carbs.

INGREDIENTS
1 mug
2 eggs
Salt and pepper
1 cup cheddar cheese, shredded
Your favorite buffalo wing sauce
INSTRUCTIONS
1. Crack the eggs into a mug and whisk until blended.
2. Put the mug into your microwave and cook for 1.5 – 2 minutes, depending on the power of your microwave.
3. Leave for a few minutes and remove from the microwave.
4. Sprinkle with salt and pepper. Add your desired amount of cheese on top.
5. Using a fork, mix everything together.
6. Then add your favorite buffalo or hot sauce and mix again.
7. Serve!

BANANA CHIA SEED PUDDING
Prep & Cook Time: 1-2 days | Servings: 1
210 cal., 12g fat, 2g protein & 5g carbs.

INGREDIENTS
2 cups coconut milk
1 banana, ripe
½ tsp. cinnamon
1 tsp. vanilla extract
¼ cup chia seeds
INSTRUCTIONS
1. In a bowl, mash the banana until soft.
2. Add the remaining ingredients and mix until incorporated.
3. Cover and place in your refrigerator overnight.
4. Serve!

STRAWBERRY RHUBARB PARFAIT
Prep & Cook Time: 1-2 days | Servings: 1
449 cal., 45g fat, 6g protein & 6g carbs.

INGREDIENTS
1 package crème fraiche or plain full-fat yogurt (8.5 oz.)
2 tbsp. almond flakes, toasted
2 tbsp. coconut flakes, toasted
6 tbsp. low-carb strawberry and rhubarb jam (4.25 oz.)
INSTRUCTIONS
1. Add the jam into a dessert bowl (3 tbsp. per serving).
2. Add the crème fraîche and garnish with the toasted almond and coconut flakes.
3. Serve!

SAUSAGE EGG MUFFINS
Prep & Cook Time: 30 minutes | Servings: 4
505 cal., 39g fat, 34g protein & 2g carbs.

INGREDIENTS
6 oz. pork sausage
6 eggs
⅛ cup heavy cream
3 oz. cheddar cheese
INSTRUCTIONS
1. Preheat the oven to 350°F/175°C.
2. Grease a muffin pan.
3. Slice the sausage links and place them two to a tin.
4. Beat the eggs with the cream and season with salt and pepper.
5. Pour over the sausages in the tin.
6. Sprinkle with cheese and the remaining egg mixture.
7. Cook for 20 minutes or until the eggs are done and serve!

SALMON OMELET
Prep & Cook Time: 15 minutes | Servings: 2
460 cal., 35g fat, 36g protein & 1.7g carbs.

INGREDIENTS
3 eggs
1 smoked salmon
3 links pork sausage
¼ cup onions
¼ cup provolone cheese
INSTRUCTIONS
1. Whisk the eggs and pour them into a skillet.
2. Pour the mixture onto a skillet on a high heat and fry for 2 – 3 minutes until browned.
3. Add the onions, salmon and cheese before turning the omelet over.
4. Sprinkle the omelet with cheese and serve with the sausages on the side.
5. Serve!

EGG PARMESAN BREAKFAST CASSEROLE
Prep & Cook Time: 40 minutes | Servings: 4
475 cal., 45g fat, 38g protein & 2.5g carbs.

INGREDIENTS
5 eggs
3 tbsp. chunky tomato sauce
2 tbsp. heavy cream
2 tbsp. parmesan cheese, grated
INSTRUCTIONS
1. Preheat your oven to 350°F/175°C.
2. Combine the eggs and cream in a bowl.
3. Mix in the tomato sauce and add the cheese.
4. Spread into a glass baking dish and bake for 25-35 minutes.
5. Top with extra cheese.
6. Enjoy!

HASH BROWNS
Prep & Cook Time: 30 minutes | Servings: 4
120 cal., 9g fat, 9g protein & 3g carbs.

INGREDIENTS
12 oz. fresh cauliflower (about ½ a medium-sized head), grated
4 slices bacon, chopped
3 oz. onion, chopped
1 tbsp. butter, softened
INSTRUCTIONS
1. In a skillet, sauté the bacon and onions on a medium heat until brown.
2. Add in the cauliflower and stir until tender and browned.
3. Add the butter steadily as it cooks.
4. Season to taste with salt and pepper.
5. Enjoy.

BACON CUPS
Prep & Cook Time: 30 minutes | Servings: 2
205 cal., 15g fat, 14g protein & 1g carbs.

INGREDIENTS
2 eggs
1 slice tomato
3 slices bacon
2 slices ham
2 tsp. parmesan cheese, grated
INSTRUCTIONS
1. Preheat your oven to 375°F/190°C.
2. Cook the bacon for half of the directed time.
3. Slice the bacon strips in half and line 2 greased muffin tins with 3 half-strips of bacon.
4. Put one slice of ham and half slice of tomato in each muffin tin on top of the bacon.
5. Crack one egg on top of the tomato in each muffin tin and sprinkle each with half a tsp. of grated parmesan cheese.
6. Bake for 20 minutes.
7. Remove and let cool.
8. Serve!

SPINACH EGGS & CHEESE
Prep & Cook Time: 40 minutes | Servings: 3
200 cal., 25g fat, 16g protein & 2g carbs.

INGREDIENTS
3 eggs
3 oz. cottage cheese
3-4 oz. spinach, chopped
¼ cup parmesan cheese
¼ cup milk
INSTRUCTIONS
1. Preheat your oven to 375°F/190°C.
2. In a large bowl, whisk the eggs, cottage cheese, the parmesan and the milk.
3. Mix in the spinach.
4. Transfer to a small, greased, oven dish.
5. Sprinkle the cheese on top.
6. Bake for 25-30 minutes.
7. Let cool for 5 minutes and serve.
8. Serve!

FRIED EGGS
Prep & Cook Time: 8 minutes | Servings: 1
220 cal., 21g fat, 12g protein & 1g carbs.

INGREDIENTS
2 eggs
3 slices bacon
INSTRUCTIONS

1. Heat some oil in a deep fryer at 375°F/190°C.
2. Fry the bacon.
3. In a small bowl, add the 2 eggs.
4. Quickly add the eggs into the center of the fryer.
5. Using two spatulas, form the egg into a ball while frying.
6. Fry for 2-3 minutes, until it stops bubbling.
7. Place on a paper towel and allow to drain.
8. Enjoy!

SCOTCH EGGS

Prep & Cook Time: 35 minutes | Servings: 2
345 cal., 28g fat, 18g protein & 2g carbs.

INGREDIENTS
4 eggs
1 link pork sausage (12 oz.)
8 slices bacon
4 toothpicks
INSTRUCTIONS
1. Hard-boil the eggs, peel the shells and let them cool.
2. Slice the sausage into four parts and place each part into a large circle.
3. Put an egg into each circle and wrap it in the sausage.
4. Place inside your refrigerator for 1 hour.
5. Make a cross with two pieces of thick cut bacon.
6. Place a wrapped egg in the center, fold the bacon over top of the egg and secure with a toothpick.
7. Cook inside your oven at 450°F/230°C for 25 minutes.
8. Enjoy!

BREAKFAST CHEESY SAUSAGE

Serves: 2 | Prep Time: 20 mins
244 cal., 20g fat, 16g protein & 1g carbs.

INGREDIENTS
2 links pork sausage, cut open and casing discarded
Sea salt & Black pepper
½ tsp. thyme
½ tsp. sage
1 cup mozzarella cheese, shredded
INSTRUCTIONS
1. Add the sea salt, sausage meat, thyme, black pepper, mozzarella cheese and sage into a bowl and mix well.
2. Form 2 equal patties out of the mixture and cook on a hot pan for 5 minutes each side.
3. Serve!

CAULIFLOWER TOAST & AVOCADO

Serves: 2 | Prep Time: 20 mins
126 cal., 7 fat, 9 protein & 9g carbs.

INGREDIENTS
1 egg
1 cauliflower head, grated
1 avocado, chopped
¾ cup mozzarella cheese, shredded
Salt & Black pepper
INSTRUCTIONS
1. Set the oven to preheat at 420°F then line the baking tray with a parchment paper.
2. Cook the cauliflower in the microwave on high for 7 minutes.

3. Allow the cauliflower to cool then drain on paper towel.
4. Remove the excess moisture by pressing with a clean kitchen towel then put them in a bowl.
5. Add the egg and mozzarella then stir.
6. Add the seasonings and mix evenly then shape the mixture into medium squares.
7. Arrange the squares on the prepared baking tray.
8. Allow to bake until browned evenly, for about 20 minutes.
9. In the meantime, puree the avocado with black pepper and salt.
10. Top with the pureed avocado.
11. Serve!

MILLENNIALS' KETO AVOCADO TOAST

Serves: 2 | Prep Time: 20 mins
140 cal., 11 fat, 10 protein & 5g carbs.

INGREDIENTS
2 tbsp. sunflower oil
½ cup parmesan cheese, shredded
1 avocado, sliced
Sea salt
4 slices cauliflower bread
INSTRUCTIONS
1. Pour the oil in a pan to heat then fry the cauliflower bread slices for 2 minutes each side.
2. Sprinkle the seasonings on the avocado and place on the cauliflower bread topped with the cheese.
3. Cook in the microwave for 2 minutes.
4. Serve!

CHOCOLATE CHIP WAFFLES

Serves: 2 | Prep Time: 30 mins
300 cal., 19 fat, 9 protein & 6.8g carbs.

INGREDIENTS
2 scoops vanilla protein powder
1 tsp. sea salt
50 grams 90% chocolate chips
2 eggs
2 tbsp. butter, melted
INSTRUCTIONS
1. Put the butter, vanilla protein powder and egg yolks in a bowl and mix well.
2. In another bowl, whisk the egg whites thoroughly then add to the vanilla mixture.
3. Gently fold in the chocolate chips and salt.
4. Cook the mixture on the waffle maker in relation to manufacturer's guidelines.
5. Serve!

EGG CREPES WITH AVOCADOS

Serves: 2 | Prep Time: 15 mins
371 cal., 6 fat, 27g protein & 9.5g carbs.

INGREDIENTS
4 eggs
¾ avocado, sliced
2 tsp. olive oil
½ cup alfalfa sprouts
4 slices turkey breast, shredded
INSTRUCTIONS

1. Pour the olive oil in a pan and heat over medium heat.
2. Crush the eggs and cook for 3 minutes each side on the pan as you spread to cook evenly.
3. Remove the eggs from heat, then top with avocado, turkey breast, sprouts and alfalfa then roll up well.
4. Serve!

HAM AND CHEESE POCKETS

Serves: 2 | Prep Time: 30 mins
360 cal., 27 fat, 24g protein & 7.8g carbs.

INGREDIENTS
1 oz. cream cheese
¾ cup mozzarella cheese, shredded
2 tbsp. flax meal
3 oz. provolone cheese slices
3 oz. ham

INSTRUCTIONS
1. Set the oven to preheat at 4000F then line a baking sheet with parchment paper.
2. Put the mozzarella cheese and cream cheese in a microwave to melt for 1 minute.
3. Add the flax meal to the melted mozzarella and mix well to form a dough.
4. Spread the dough and roll evenly.
5. Top the provolone cheese slices and ham on the rolled dough.
6. Shape the dough into an envelope-like shape.
7. Close the edges and make some holes in it.
8. Arrange them well on the baking tray and put in the oven.
9. Allow baking for 20 minutes then remove from the oven to cool.
10. Slice halt way.
11. Serve!

CLEMENTINE & PISTACHIO RICOTTA

Serves: 2 | Prep Time: 10 mins
311 cal., 30 fat, 11g protein & 13g carbs.

INGREDIENTS
2 tsp. pistachios, chopped
¾ cup ricotta
4 strawberries
1 tbsp. butter, melted
2 segmented clementine

INSTRUCTIONS
1. Have 2 serving bowls then put equal amounts of ricotta in each bowl.
2. Add the strawberries, butter, pistachios and clementine segments to serve.
3. Serve!

CHIPOTLE JICAMA HASH

Prep & Cook Time: 15 minutes | Servings: 2
265 cal., 23g fat, 19g protein & 11g carbs.

INGREDIENTS
4 slices bacon, chopped
12 oz. jicama, peeled & diced
4 oz. red onion, chopped
1 oz. green bell pepper (or poblano), seeded & chopped
4 tbsp. chipotle mayonnaise

INSTRUCTIONS
1. In a skillet, brown the bacon on a high heat.
2. Remove and place on a towel to drain the grease.
3. Use the remaining grease to fry the onions and jicama until brown.
4. When ready, add the bell pepper and cook the hash until tender.
5. Transfer the hash onto two plates and serve each plate with 4 tbsp. of Chipotle mayonnaise.

FRIED QUESO BLANCO

Prep & Cook Time: 170 minutes | Servings: 4
307 cal., 24g fat, 17g protein & 3g carbs.

INGREDIENTS
5 oz. queso blanco
1 ½ tbsp. olive oil
3 oz. cheddar cheese
2 oz. olives
1 pinch red pepper flakes

INSTRUCTIONS
1. Cube some cheese and freeze it for 1-2 hours.
2. Pour the oil in a skillet and heat to boil over a medium temperature.
3. Add the cheese cubes and heat till brown.
4. Combine the cheese together using a spatula and flatten.
5. Cook the cheese on both sides, flipping regularly.
6. While flipping, fold the cheese into itself to form crispy layers.
7. Use a spatula to roll it into a block.
8. Remove it from the pan, allow it to cool, cut it into small cubes, and serve.

SPINACH WITH BACON & SHALLOTS

Prep & Cook Time: 30 minutes | Servings: 4
150 cal., 13g fat, 4g protein & 5g carbs.

INGREDIENTS
16 oz. raw spinach
½ cup onion, chopped
½ cup shallot, chopped
½ lb. bacon slices
2 tbsp. butter

INSTRUCTIONS
1. Slice the bacon strips into small narrow pieces.
2. In a skillet, heat the butter and add the chopped onion, shallots and bacon.
3. Sauté for 15-20 minutes or until the onions start to caramelize and the bacon is cooked.
4. Add the spinach and sauté on a medium heat. Stir frequently to ensure the leaves touch the skillet while cooking.
5. Cover and steam for around 5 minutes, stir and continue until wilted.
6. Serve!

BACON-WRAPPED SAUSAGE SKEWERS

Prep & Cook Time: 8 minutes | Servings: 2
290 cal., 22g fat, 8g protein & 1g carbs.

INGREDIENTS
1 link pork sausage

10 slices bacon
INSTRUCTIONS
1. Preheat your deep fryer to 370°F/190°C.
2. Cut the sausage into four pieces.
3. Slice the bacon in half.
4. Wrap the bacon over the sausage.
5. Skewer the sausage.
6. Fry for 4-5 minutes until browned.

ROASTED BRUSSELS SPROUTS & BACON
Prep & Cook Time: 45 minutes | Servings: 2
130 cal., 9g fat, 7g protein & 5g carbs.

INGREDIENTS
24 oz. brussels sprouts
¼ cup fish sauce
¼ cup bacon grease
6 strips bacon
Pepper to taste
INSTRUCTIONS
1. De-stem and quarter the brussels sprouts.
2. Mix them with the bacon grease and fish sauce.
3. Slice the bacon into small strips and cook.
4. Add the bacon and pepper to the sprouts.
5. Spread onto a greased pan and cook at 450°F/230°C for 35 minutes.
6. Stir every 5 minute or so.
7. Broil for a few more minutes and serve.

HAM & CHEESE ROLLS
Prep & Cook Time: 5 minutes | Servings: 4
200 cal., 12g fat, 16g protein & 3g carbs.

INGREDIENTS
16 slices ham
1 package chive and onion cream cheese (8 oz.)
16 slices thin Swiss cheese
INSTRUCTIONS
1. Place the ham on a chopping board.
2. Dry the slices with a paper towel.
3. Thinly spread 2 tsp. of Swiss cheese over each slice of ham.
4. On the clean section of ham, add a half inch slice of cheese.
5. On the cheese side, fold the ham over the cheese and roll it up.
6. Leave it as is, or slice into smaller rolls.

HILLBILLY CHEESE SURPRISE
Prep & Cook Time: 40 minutes | Servings: 6
436 cal., 38g fat, 12g protein & 4g carbs.

INGREDIENTS
4 cups broccoli florets
¼ cup ranch dressing
½ cup sharp cheddar cheese, shredded
¼ cup heavy cream
Kosher salt & pepper to taste
INSTRUCTIONS
1. Preheat your oven to 375°F/190°C.
2. In a bowl, combine all of the ingredients until the broccoli is well-covered.
3. In a casserole dish, spread out the broccoli mixture.

4. Bake for 30 minutes.
5. Take out of your oven and mix.
6. If the florets are not tender, bake for another 5 minutes until tender.
7. Serve!

PARMESAN & GARLIC CAULIFLOWER
Prep & Cook Time: 40 minutes | Servings: 4
180 cal., 18g fat, 7g protein & 6g carbs.

INGREDIENTS
¾ cup cauliflower floret
2 tbsp. butter
1 clove garlic, sliced
2 tbsp. parmesan cheese, shredded
1 pinch salt
INSTRUCTIONS
1. Preheat your oven to 350°F/175°C.
2. On a low heat, melt the butter with the garlic for 5-10 minutes.
3. Strain the garlic in a sieve.
4. Add the cauliflower, parmesan and salt.
5. Bake for 20 minutes or until golden.

JALAPEÑO GUACAMOLE
Prep & Cook Time: 30 minutes | Servings: 4
130 cal., 10g fat, 3g protein & 9g carbs.

INGREDIENTS
2 avocados, ripe
¼ red onion
1 jalapeño
1 tbsp. fresh lime juice
Sea salt to taste
INSTRUCTIONS
1. Spoon the avocado innings into a bowl.
2. Dice the jalapeño and onion.
3. Mash the avocado to the desired consistency.
4. Add in the onion, jalapeño and lime juice.
5. Sprinkle with salt.

GREEN BEANS & ALMONDS
Prep & Cook Time: 15 minutes | Servings: 4
178 cal., 16g fat, 4g protein & 4g carbs.

INGREDIENTS
1 lb. fresh green beans, trimmed
2 tbsp. butter
¼ cup almonds, sliced
2 tsp. lemon pepper
INSTRUCTIONS
1. Steam the green beans for 8 minutes, until tender, then drain.
2. On a medium heat, melt the butter in a skillet.
3. Sauté the almonds until browned.
4. Sprinkle with salt and pepper.
5. Mix in the green beans.

SUGAR SNAP BACON
Prep & Cook Time: 10 minutes | Servings: 4
80 cal., 4g fat, 3g protein & 1g carbs.

INGREDIENTS
3 cups sugar snap peas
½ tbsp. lemon juice
2 tbsp. bacon fat
2 tsp. garlic
½ tsp. red pepper flakes
INSTRUCTIONS
1. In a skillet, cook the bacon fat until it begins to smoke.
2. Add the garlic and cook for 2 minutes.
3. Add the sugar peas and lemon juice.
4. Cook for 2-3 minutes.
5. Remove and sprinkle with red pepper flakes and lemon zest.
6. Serve!

FLAX CHEESE CHIPS
Prep & Cook Time: 20 minutes | Servings: 2
130 cal., 8g fat, 5g protein & 1g carbs.

INGREDIENTS
1 ½ cup cheddar cheese
4 tbsp. ground flaxseed meal
Seasonings of your choice
INSTRUCTIONS
1. Preheat your oven to 425°F/220°C.
2. Spoon 2 tbsp. of cheddar cheese into a mound, onto a non-stick pad.
3. Spread out a pinch of flax seed on each chip.
4. Season and bake for 10-15 minutes.

COUNTRY STYLE CHARD
Prep & Cook Time: 5 minutes | Servings: 2
190 cal., 4g fat, 5g protein & 10g carbs.

INGREDIENTS
4 slices bacon, chopped
2 tbsp. butter
2 tbsp. fresh lemon juice
½ tsp. garlic paste
1 bunch Swiss chard, stems removed, leaves cut into 1-inch pieces
INSTRUCTIONS
1. On a medium heat, cook the bacon in a skillet until the fat begins to brown.
2. Melt the butter in the skillet and add the lemon juice and garlic paste.
3. Add the chard leaves and cook until they begin to wilt.
4. Cover and turn up the heat to high.
5. Cook for 3 minutes.
6. Mix well, sprinkle with salt and serve.

KALE CRISPS
Prep & Cook Time: 15 minutes | Servings: 1
60 cal., 3g fat, 2g protein & 2g carbs.

INGREDIENTS
1 large bunch kale
2 tbsp. olive oil
1 tbsp. salt
INSTRUCTIONS
1. Preheat your oven to 350°F/175°C.
2. De-stem, wash and dry the kale.
3. Put it inside a Ziploc bag and shake with oil.

4. Put the kale on a baking sheet.
5. Bake for 10 minutes.
6. Remove and serve hot!

BAKED TORTILLAS
Prep & Cook Time: 30 minutes | Servings: 4
89 cal., 6g fat, 3g protein & 4g carbs.

INGREDIENTS
1 head cauliflower, divided into florets.
4 eggs
2 garlic cloves, minced
1 ½ tsp. herbs (whatever your favorite is basil, oregano, thyme)
½ tsp. salt
INSTRUCTIONS
1. Preheat your oven to 375°F/190°C.
2. Put parchment paper on two baking sheets.
3. In a food processor, break down the cauliflower into rice.
4. Add ¼ cup water and the riced cauliflower to a saucepan.
5. Cook on a medium high heat until tender for 10 minutes. Drain.
6. Dry with a clean kitchen towel.
7. Mix the cauliflower, eggs, garlic, herbs and salt.
8. Make 4 thin circles on the parchment paper.
9. Bake for 20 minutes, until dry.

HOMEMADE MAYONNAISE
Prep & Cook Time: 30 minutes | Servings: 4
95 cal., 9g fat, 9g protein & 1g carbs.

INGREDIENTS
1 egg
Juice from 1 lemon
1 tsp. dry mustard
½ tsp. black pepper
1 cup avocado oil
INSTRUCTIONS
1. Combine the egg and lemon juice in a container and let sit for 20 minutes.
2. Add the dry mustard, pepper, and avocado oil.
3. Insert an electric whisk into the container.
4. Blend for 30 seconds.
5. Transfer to a sealed container and store in your refrigerator.

HOLLANDAISE SAUCE
Prep & Cook Time: 2 minutes | Servings: 8 95 cal., 50g fat, 3g protein & 1g carbs.

INGREDIENTS
8 large, emulsified egg yolks
½ tsp. salt
2 tbsp. fresh lemon juice
1 cup butter, unsalted
INSTRUCTIONS
1. Combine the egg yolks, salt, and lemon juice in a blender until smooth.
2. Put the butter in your microwave for around 60 seconds, until melted and hot.

3. Turn the blender on a low speed and slowly pour in the butter until the sauce begins to thicken.
4. Serve!

- -

GARLICKY GREEN BEANS
Prep & Cook Time: 10 minutes | Servings: 4
215 cal., 9g fat, 4g protein & 7g carbs.

INGREDIENTS
1 lb. green beans, trimmed
1 cup butter
2 cloves garlic, minced
1 cup pine nuts, toasted
INSTRUCTIONS
1. Boil a pot of water.
2. Add the green beans and cook until tender for 5 minutes.
3. Heat the butter in a large skillet over a high heat. Add the garlic and pine nuts and sauté for 2 minutes or until the pine nuts are lightly browned.
4. Transfer the green beans to the skillet and turn until coated.
5. Serve.

- -

MONKEY SALAD
Prep & Cook Time: 10 minutes | Servings: 8
295 cal., 22g fat, 4g protein & 4g carbs.

INGREDIENTS
2 tbsp. butter
1 cup coconut flakes, unsweetened
1 cup raw, unsalted cashews
1 cup raw, unsalted almonds
1 banana (optional), chopped
1 cup 90% dark chocolate shavings

INSTRUCTIONS
1. In a skillet, melt the butter on a medium heat.
2. Add the coconut flakes and sauté until lightly browned for 4 minutes.
3. Add the cashews and almonds and sauté for 3 minutes. Remove from the heat and sprinkle with dark chocolate shavings.
4. Add salt, chopped banana to taste.
5. Serve!

- -

JARLSBERG LUNCH OMELET
Prep & Cook Time: 10 minutes | Servings: 2
525 cal., 37g fat, 40g protein & 2g carbs.

INGREDIENTS
4 mushrooms, sliced
1 onion, sliced
2 eggs, beaten
1 oz. Jarlsberg or Swiss cheese, shredded
1 oz. ham, diced
INSTRUCTIONS
1. In a skillet, cook the mushrooms and green onion until tender.
2. Add the eggs and mix well.
3. Sprinkle with salt and top with the mushroom mixture, cheese and the ham.

4. When the egg is set, fold the plain side of the omelet on the filled side.
5. Turn off the heat and let it stand until the cheese has melted.
6. Serve!

- -

MU SHU LUNCH PORK
Prep & Cook Time: 10 minutes | Servings: 4
550 cal., 10g fat, 30g protein & 16g carbs.

INGREDIENTS
4 cups coleslaw mix, with carrots
1 onion, sliced
1 lb. cooked roast pork, cut into ½ cubes
2 tbsp. hoisin sauce
2 tbsp. soy sauce
INSTRUCTIONS
1. In a large skillet, heat the oil on a high heat.
2. Stir-fry the cabbage and onion for 4 minutes until tender.
3. Add the pork, hoisin and soy sauce.
4. Cook until browned.
5. Enjoy!

- -

FIERY JALAPENO POPPERS
Prep & Cook Time: 40 minutes | Servings: 4
550 cal., 12g fat, 25g protein & 5g carbs.

INGREDIENTS
5 oz. cream cheese
¼ cup mozzarella cheese
8 medium jalapeno peppers
½ tsp. Mrs. Dash Table Blend
8 slices bacon
INSTRUCTIONS
1. Preheat your oven to 400°F/200°C.
2. Cut the jalapenos in half.
3. Use a spoon to scrape out the insides of the peppers.
4. In a bowl, add together the cream cheese, mozzarella cheese and spices of your choice.
5. Pack the cream cheese mixture into the jalapenos and place the peppers on top.
6. Wrap each pepper in 1 slice of bacon, starting from the bottom and working up.
7. Bake for 30 minutes. Broil for an additional 3 minutes.
8. Serve!

- -

BACON & CHICKEN PATTIES
Prep & Cook Time: 15 minutes | Servings: 2
420 cal., 22g fat, 37g protein & 4g carbs.

INGREDIENTS
1 ½ oz. chicken breasts
4 slices bacon
¼ cup parmesan cheese
1 egg
3 tbsp. coconut flour
INSTRUCTIONS
1. Cook the bacon until crispy.
2. Chop the chicken and bacon together in a food processor until fine.
3. Add in the parmesan, egg, coconut flour and mix.

4. Make the patties by hand and fry on a medium heat in a pan with some oil.
5. Once browned, flip over, continue cooking, and lie them to drain.
6. Serve!

CHEDDAR BACON BURST
Prep & Cook Time: 90 minutes | Servings: 8
430 cal., 33g fat, 26g protein & 3g carbs.

INGREDIENTS
30 slices bacon
½ cups cheddar cheese
4-5 cups raw spinach
1-2 tbsp. Tones Southwest Chipotle Seasoning
2 tsp. Mrs. Dash Table Seasoning
INSTRUCTIONS
1. Preheat your oven to 375°F/190°C.
2. Weave the bacon into 15 vertical pieces & 12 horizontal pieces. Cut the extra 3 in half to fill in the rest, horizontally.
3. Season the bacon.
4. Add the cheese to the bacon.
5. Add the spinach and press down to compress.
6. Tightly roll up the woven bacon.
7. Line a baking sheet with kitchen foil and add plenty of salt to it.
8. Put the bacon on top of a cooling rack and put that on top of your baking sheet.
9. Bake for 60-70 minutes.
10. Let cool for 10-15 minutes before
11. Slice and enjoy!

GRILLED HAM & CHEESE
Prep & Cook Time: 30 minutes | Servings: 3
230 cal., 21g fat, 15g protein & 2g carbs.

INGREDIENTS
4 slices ham
1 tbsp. butter
3 slices cheddar cheese
½ cup almond flour
1 tsp. baking powder
4 eggs, scrambled
½ tbsp. coconut flour
INSTRUCTIONS
1. Preheat your oven to 350°F/175°C.
2. Mix the almond flour, salt and baking powder in a bowl. Put to the side.
3. Add in the butter and coconut oil to a skillet. Melt for 20 seconds and pour into another bowl.
4. In this bowl, mix in the dough.
5. Scramble two eggs. Add to the dough.
6. Add ½ tbsp. of coconut flour to thicken, and place evenly into a cupcake tray. Fill about ¾ inch.
7. Bake for 20 minutes until browned.
8. Allow to cool for 15 minutes and cut each in half for the buns.
9. Sandwich:
10. Fry the deli meat in a skillet on a high heat.
11. Put the ham and cheese between the buns. Heat the butter on medium high.
12. When brown, turn to low and add the dough to pan.
13. Press down with a weight until you smell burning, then flip to crisp both sides.

PROSCIUTTO SPINACH SALAD
Prep & Cook Time: 5 minutes | Servings: 2
199 cal., 18g fat, 6.5g protein & 2.5g carbs.

INGREDIENTS
1 cup baby spinach
⅓ lb. prosciutto
½ cantaloupe
1 avocado
¼ cup red onion, diced
handful of raw, unsalted walnuts
INSTRUCTIONS
1. Put a cup of spinach on each plate.
2. Top with the diced prosciutto, cubes of balls of melon, slices of avocado, a handful of red onion and a few walnuts.
3. Add some freshly ground pepper, if you like.
4. Serve!

RICED CAULIFLOWER & CURRY CHICKEN
Prep & Cook Time: 30 minutes | Servings: 6
950 cal., 45g fat, 31g protein & 8g carbs.

INGREDIENTS
2 lb. chicken (4 breasts)
1 packet curry paste
3 tbsp. ghee (can substitute with butter)
½ cup heavy cream
1 head cauliflower (around 1 kg)
INSTRUCTIONS
1. In a large skillet, melt the ghee.
2. Add the curry paste and mix.
3. Once combined, add a cup of water and simmer for 5 minutes.
4. Add the chicken, cover the skillet and simmer for 18 minutes.
5. Cut a cauliflower head into florets and blend in a food processor to make the riced cauliflower.
6. Cook the cauliflower inside a pan with water on the stove top, simmer until soft.
7. When the chicken is cooked, uncover, add the cream and cook for an additional 7 minutes.
8. Serve!

MASHED GARLIC TURNIPS
Prep & Cook Time: 10 minutes | Servings: 2
150 cal., 14g fat, 3g protein & 4g carbs.

INGREDIENTS
3 cups turnip, diced
2 cloves garlic, minced
¼ cup heavy cream
3 tbsp. butter, melted
Salt & pepper to season
INSTRUCTIONS
1. Boil the turnips until tender.
2. Drain and mash the turnips.
3. Add the cream, butter, salt, pepper and garlic. Combine well.
4. Serve!

LASAGNA-STYLE SPAGHETTI SQUASH

Prep & Cook Time: 90 minutes | Servings: 6
420 cal., 31g fat, 25g protein & 5g carbs.

INGREDIENTS
25 slices mozzarella cheese
1 large jar (40 oz.) Rao's Marinara sauce
30 oz. whole-milk ricotta cheese
1 large spaghetti squash, cooked (44 oz.)
1 lb. ground beef

INSTRUCTIONS
1. Preheat your oven to 375°F/190°C.
2. Slice the spaghetti squash and place it face down inside an oven proof dish. Fill with water until covered.
3. Bake for 45 minutes until skin is soft.
4. Sear the meat until browned.
5. In a large skillet, heat the browned meat and marinara sauce. Set aside when warm.
6. Scrape the flesh off the cooked squash to resemble strands of spaghetti.
7. Layer the lasagna in a large, greased pan in alternating layers of spaghetti squash, meat sauce, mozzarella, ricotta. Repeat until all increased have been used.
8. Bake for 30 minutes and serve!

BLUE CHEESE CHICKEN WEDGES
Prep & Cook Time: 45 minutes | Servings: 4
315 cal., 22g fat, 19g protein & 8g carbs.

INGREDIENTS
Blue cheese dressing
2 tbsp. crumbled blue cheese
4 strips bacon
2 chicken breasts (boneless)
¾ cup of your favorite buffalo sauce

INSTRUCTIONS
1. Boil a large pot of salted water.
2. Add in two chicken breasts to pot and cook for 28 minutes.
3. Turn off the heat and let the chicken rest for 10 minutes. Using a fork, pull the chicken apart into strips.
4. Cook and cool the bacon strips and put to the side.
5. On a medium heat, combine the chicken and buffalo sauce. Stir until hot.
6. Add the blue cheese and buffalo pulled chicken. Top with the cooked bacon crumble.
7. Serve and enjoy.

'OH, SO GOOD' SALAD
Prep & Cook Time: 10 minutes | Servings: 2
110 cal., 10g fat, 4g protein & 2g carbs.

INGREDIENTS
6 brussels sprouts
½ tsp. apple cider vinegar
1 tsp. olive/grapeseed oil
1 pinch salt
1 tbsp. parmesan cheese, grated

INSTRUCTIONS
1. Slice the clean brussels sprouts in half.
2. Cut thin slices in the opposite direction.
3. Once sliced, cut the roots off and discard.
4. Toss together with the apple cider, oil and salt.
5. Sprinkle with the parmesan cheese, combine and enjoy!

'I LOVE BACON
Prep & Cook Time: 90 minutes | Servings: 4
388 cal., 38g fat, 29g protein & 3g carbs.

INGREDIENTS
30 slices bacon
12 oz. steak
10 oz. pork sausage
4 oz. cheddar cheese, shredded

INSTRUCTIONS
1. Lay out 5 x 6 slices of bacon in a woven pattern and bake at 400°F/200°C for 20 minutes until crisp.
2. Combine the steak, bacon and sausage to form a meaty mixture.
3. Lay out the meat in a rectangle of similar size to the bacon strips. Season with salt/pepper.
4. Place the bacon weave on top of the meat mixture.
5. Place the cheese in the center of the bacon.
6. Roll the meat into a tight roll and refrigerate.
7. Make a 7 x 7 bacon weave and roll the bacon weave over the meat, diagonally.
8. Bake at 400°F/200°C for 60 minutes or 165°F/75°C internally.
9. Let rest for 5 minutes before serving.

LEMON DILL TROUT
Prep & Cook Time: 10 minutes | Servings: 1
460 cal., 22g fat, 57g protein & 1g carbs.

INGREDIENTS
2 lb. pan-dressed trout (or other small fish), fresh or frozen
1 ½ tsp. salt
½ cup butter
2 tbsp. dill weed
3 tbsp. lemon juice

INSTRUCTIONS
1. Cut the fish lengthwise and season the with pepper.
2. Prepare a skillet by melting the butter and dill weed.
3. Fry the fish on a high heat, flesh side down, for 2-3 minutes per side.
4. Remove the fish. Add the lemon juice to the butter and dill to create a sauce.
5. Serve the fish with the sauce.

NO POTATO SHEPHERD'S PIE
Prep & Cook Time: 70 minutes | Servings: 6
480 cal., 28g fat, 12g protein & 10g carbs.

INGREDIENTS
1 lb. ground beef
8 oz. low-carb mushroom sauce mix
¼ cup ketchup
1 lb. frozen mixed vegetables
1 lb. Aitkin's low carb bake mix or equivalent

INSTRUCTIONS
1. Preheat your oven to 375°F/190°C.
2. Prepare the bake mix according to package instructions. Layer into the skillet base.
3. Brown the ground beef with the salt. Stir in the mushroom sauce, ketchup and mixed vegetables.
4. Bring the mixture to the boil and reduce the heat to medium, cover and simmer until tender.

5. Bake until piping hot and serve!

EASY SLIDER
Prep & Cook Time: 70 minutes | Servings: 6
419 cal., 35g fat, 20g protein & 8g carbs.

INGREDIENTS
½ lb. ground beef
5 eggs
Garlic/salt/pepper/onion powder to taste
Several dashes of Worcestershire sauce
8 oz. cheddar cheese (½ oz. per patty)
INSTRUCTIONS
1. Mix the beef, eggs and spices together.
2. Divide the meat into 1.5 oz. patties.
3. Add a half-ounce of cheese to each patty and combine two patties to make one burger, like a sandwich. Heat the oil on high and fry the burgers until cooked as desired.
4. Serve.

DIJON HALIBUT STEAK
Prep & Cook Time: 20 minutes | Servings: 1
305 cal., 16g fat, 34g protein & 6g carbs.

INGREDIENTS
1 6-oz. halibut steak, thawed
1 tbsp. butter
1 tbsp. lemon juice
½ tbsp. Dijon mustard
1 tsp. fresh basil
INSTRUCTIONS
1. Heat the butter, basil, lemon juice and mustard in a small saucepan to make a glaze.
2. Brush both sides of the halibut steak with the mixture.
3. Grill the fish for 10 minutes over a medium heat until tender and flakey.

CAST-IRON CHEESY CHICKEN
Prep & Cook Time: 10 minutes | Servings: 4
419 cal., 29g fat, 32g protein & 2g carbs.

INGREDIENTS
4 chicken breasts
4 bacon strips
4 oz. ranch dressing
2 onions
4 oz. cheddar cheese
INSTRUCTIONS
1. Pour the oil into a skillet and heat on high. Add the chicken breasts and fry both sides until piping hot.
2. Fry the bacon and crumble it into bits.
3. Dice the green onions.
4. Put the chicken in a baking dish and top with soy sauce.
5. Toss in the ranch, bacon, green onions and top with cheese.
6. Cook until the cheese is browned, for around 4 minutes.
7. Serve.

CAULIFLOWER RICE CHICKEN CURRY
Prep & Cook Time: 40 minutes | Servings: 4
249 cal., 18g fat, 15g protein & 6g carbs.

INGREDIENTS
2 lb. chicken (4 breasts)
1 pack curry paste
3 tbsp. ghee (can substitute with butter)
½ cup heavy cream
1 head cauliflower (around 1 kg/2.2 lb.)
INSTRUCTIONS
1. Melt the ghee in a pot. Mix in the curry paste.
2. Add the water and simmer for 5 minutes.
3. Add the chicken, cover, and simmer on a medium heat for 20 minutes or until the chicken is cooked.
4. Shred the cauliflower florets in a food processor to resemble rice.
5. Transfer the cauliflower rice into a bowl filled with water. Simmer on the stove top until soft.
6. Once the chicken is cooked, uncover, and incorporate the cream.
7. Cook for 7 minutes and serve over the cauliflower.

BACON CHOPS
Prep & Cook Time: 20 minutes | Servings: 2
439 cal., 39g fat, 12g protein & 9g carbs.

INGREDIENTS
2 pork chops (I prefer bone-in, but boneless chops work great as well)
1 bag shredded brussels sprouts
4 slices bacon
Worcestershire sauce
Lemon juice (optional)
INSTRUCTIONS
1. Place the pork chops on a baking sheet with the Worcestershire sauce inside a preheated grill for 5 minutes.
2. Turnover and cook for another 5 minutes. Put to the side when done.
3. Cook the chopped bacon in a large pan until browned. Add the shredded brussels sprouts and cook together.
4. Stir the brussels sprouts with the bacon and grease and cook for 5 minutes until the bacon is crisp.

CHICKEN IN A BLANKET
Prep & Cook Time: 60 minutes | Servings: 3
380 cal., 29g fat, 11g protein & 3g carbs.

INGREDIENTS
3 boneless chicken breasts
3 strips bacon
1 8-oz. cream cheese
3 jalapeno peppers
Salt, pepper, garlic powder or other seasonings
INSTRUCTIONS
1. Cut the chicken breast in half lengthwise to create two pieces.
2. Cut the jalapenos in half lengthwise and remove the seeds.
3. Dress each breast with a half-inch slice of cream cheese and half a slice of jalapeno. Sprinkle with garlic powder, salt and pepper.
4. Roll the chicken and wrap 2 to 3 pieces of bacon around it—secure with toothpicks.
5. Bake in a preheated 375°F/190°C oven for 50 minutes.

6. Serve!

STUFFED CHICKEN ROLLS

Prep & Cook Time: 45 minutes | Servings: 4
270 cal., 11g fat, 38g protein & 1g carbs.

INGREDIENTS
4 chicken breasts
7 oz. cream cheese
¼ cup onions, chopped
4 slices bacon, partially cooked

INSTRUCTIONS
1. Partially cook your strips of bacon, about 5 minutes for each side and set aside.
2. Pound the chicken breasts to a quarterinch thick.
3. Mix the cream cheese and green onions together. Spread 2 tbsp. of the mixture onto each breast. Roll and wrap them with the strip of bacon, then secure with a toothpick.
4. Place the chicken on a baking sheet and bake in a preheated oven at
5. 375°F/190°C for 30 minutes.
6. Broil for 5 minutes to crisp the bacon.
7. Serve.

DUCK FAT RIBEYE

Prep & Cook Time: 20 minutes | Servings: 1
740 cal., 65g fat, 37g protein & 1g carbs

INGREDIENTS
16-oz. ribeye steak (1 - 1 ¼ inch thick)
1 tbsp. duck fat (or other high smoke point oil like peanut oil)
½ tbsp. butter
½ tsp. thyme, chopped
Salt and pepper to taste

INSTRUCTIONS
1. Preheat a skillet in your oven at 400°F/200°C.
2. Season the steaks with the oil, salt and pepper. Remove the skillet from the oven once pre-heated.
3. Put the skillet on your stove top burner on a medium heat and drizzle in the oil.
4. Sear the steak for 1-4 minutes, depending on if you like it rare, medium or well done.
5. Turn over the steak and place in your oven for 6 minutes.
6. Take out the steak from your oven and place it back on the stove top on low heat.
7. Toss in the butter and thyme and cook for 3 minutes, basting as you go along.
8. Rest for 5 minutes and serve.

EASY ZOODLES & TURKEY BALLS

Prep & Cook Time: 35 minutes | Servings: 2
287 cal., 14g fat, 24g protein & 10g carbs

INGREDIENTS
1 zucchini, cut into spirals
1 can vodka pasta sauce
1 pack frozen Armour Turkey meatballs

INSTRUCTIONS
1. Cook the meatballs and sauce on a high heat for 25 minutes, stirring occasionally.
2. Wash the zucchini and put through a vegetable spiral maker.
3. Boil the water and blanch the raw zoodles for 60 seconds. Remove and drain.
4. Combine the zoodles and prepared saucy meatballs.
5. Serve!

SAUSAGE BALLS

Prep & Cook Time: 25 minutes | Servings: 6
365 cal., 30g fat, 21g protein & 5g carbs

INGREDIENTS
12 oz. pork sausage
6 oz. cheddar cheese, shredded
10 cubes cheddar (optional)

INSTRUCTIONS
1. Mix the shredded cheese and sausage.
2. Divide the mixture into 12 equal parts to be stuffed.
3. Add a cube of cheese to the center of the sausage and roll into balls.
4. Fry at 375°F/190°C until crisp.
5. Serve!

BACON SCALLOPS

Prep & Cook Time: 10 minutes | Servings: 6
280 cal., 18g fat, 28g protein & 3g carbs

INGREDIENTS
12 scallops
12 bacon slices
12 toothpicks
Salt and pepper to taste
½ tbsp. oil

INSTRUCTIONS
1. Heat a skillet on a high heat while drizzling in the oil.
2. Wrap each scallop with a piece of thinly cut bacon— secure with a toothpick.
3. Season to taste.
4. Cook for 3 minutes per side.
5. Serve!

GLUTEN FREE GRATIN

Prep & Cook Time: 30 minutes | Servings: 2
175 cal., 15g fat, 5g protein & 2g carbs

INGREDIENTS
4 cups cauliflower florets, raw
4 tbsp. butter
⅓ cup heavy cream
Salt and pepper to taste
5 slices pepper jack cheese

INSTRUCTIONS
1. Combine the cauliflower, butter, cream, salt and pepper and microwave on medium for 20 minutes, or until tender.
2. Mash with a fork. Season to your liking.
3. Lay the slices of cheese across the top of the cauliflower.
4. Cook inside your microwave for an additional 3 minutes, depending on the power of your microwave.
5. Serve!

BUFFALO CHICKEN SALAD

Prep & Cook Time: 40 minutes | Servings: 1
410 cal., 9g fat, 15g protein & 10g carbs

INGREDIENTS

3 cups salad of your choice
1 chicken breast
½ cup shredded cheese
Buffalo wing sauce of your choice
Ranch or blue cheese dressing

INSTRUCTIONS

1. Preheat your oven to 400°F/200°C.
2. Douse the chicken breast in the buffalo wing sauce and bake for 25 minutes. In the last 5 minutes, throw the cheese on the wings until it melts.
3. When cooked, remove from the oven and slice into pieces.
4. Place on a bed of lettuce.
5. Pour the salad dressing of your choice on top.
6. Serve!

MEDITERRANEAN TURKEY CUTLETS

Serves: 2 | Prep Time: 25 mins
283 cal., 13g fat, 10g protein & 6g carbs

INGREDIENTS

1 tbsp. olive oil
½ lb. turkey cutlets
¼ cup almond flour
½ tsp. Greek seasoning
½ tsp. turmeric powder

INSTRUCTIONS

1. In a medium bowl, mix the turkey cutlets with turmeric powder, almond flour, and Greek seasoning.
2. Heat a frying pan on the stovetop then add the oil to heat.
3. Add the cutlets and cook for 5 minutes on each side under medium-low heat.
4. Serve!

MEATBALLS

Prep & Cook Time: 30 minutes | Servings: 6
380 cal., 22g fat, 18g protein & 1g carbs

INGREDIENTS

1 lb. ground beef (or ½ lb. beef, ½ lb. pork)
½ cup parmesan cheese, grated
1 tbsp. minced garlic (or paste)
½ cup mozzarella cheese
1 tsp. ground pepper

INSTRUCTIONS

1. Preheat your oven to 400°F/200°C.
2. In a bowl, mix all the ingredients together.
3. Roll the meat mixture into 6 generous meatballs.
4. Bake inside your oven at 170°F/80°C for about 18 minutes. 5. Serve with sauce!

CHICKEN TENDERS

Prep & Cook Time: 40 minutes | Servings: 3
340 cal., 25g fat, 20g protein & 2g carbs

INGREDIENTS

3 boneless, skinless chicken breasts

(thawed)
1 4-oz. bag spicy pork rinds/chicharrones
2 eggs

INSTRUCTIONS

1. Preheat your oven to 400°F/200°C.
2. Blend the pork rinds into small pieces and place onto a plate.
3. In a bowl, crack the eggs and whisk until mixed.
4. Slice the chicken breasts into 1x2 inch pieces.
5. One at a time, dip the pieces into the egg mixture and place on top of the crushed pork rinds.
6. Roll the pieces around until covered in the rind coating.
7. Put the chicken strips into an oven proof dish and bake for 28 minutes.
8. Serve!

FAT BOMBS

Prep & Cook Time: 100 minutes | Servings: 2
205 cal., 30g fat, 18g protein & 1g carbs

INGREDIENTS

1 cup coconut butter
1 cup coconut milk (full fat, canned)
1 tsp. vanilla extract (gluten free)
½ tsp. nutmeg
½ cup coconut shreds

INSTRUCTIONS

1. Pour some water into pot and put a glass bowl on top.
2. Add all the ingredients except the shredded coconut into the glass bowl and cook on a medium heat.
3. Stir and melt until they start melting.
4. Then, take them off of the heat.
5. Put the glass bowl into your refrigerator until the mix can be rolled into doughy balls. Usually this happens after around 30 minutes.
6. Roll the dough into 1-inch balls through the coconut shreds.
7. Place the balls on a plate and refrigerate for one hour.
8. Serve!

BEEF CASSEROLE

Prep & Cook Time: 40 minutes | Servings: 2
275 cal., 19g fat, 19g protein & 6g carbs

INGREDIENTS

½ lb. ground beef
½ cup onion, chopped
½ bag coleslaw mix
1-1/2 cups tomato sauce
1 tbsp. lemon juice

INSTRUCTIONS

1. In a skillet, cook the ground beef until browned and to the side.
2. Mix in the onion to the skillet and sauté until soft.
3. Add the ground beef back in along with the tomato sauce and lemon juice.
4. Bring the mixture to a boil, then cover and simmer for 30 minutes.
5. Enjoy!

ROAST BEEF LETTUCE WRAPS

Prep & Cook Time: 10 minutes | Servings: 4
460 cal., 29g fat, 32g protein & 10g carbs

INGREDIENTS
8 large iceberg lettuce leaves
8 oz. (8 slices) roast beef
½ cup homemade mayonnaise
8 slices provolone cheese
1 cup baby spinach
INSTRUCTIONS
1. Wash the lettuce leaves and sake them dry. Try not to rip them.
2. Place 1 slice of roast beef inside each wrap.
3. Smother 1 tbsp. of mayonnaise on top of each piece of roast beef.
4. Top the mayonnaise with 1 slice of provolone cheese and 1 cup of baby spinach.
5. Roll the lettuce up around the toppings.
6. Serve & enjoy!

- -

TURKEY AVOCADO ROLLS
Prep & Cook Time: 10 minutes | Servings: 6
150 cal., 9g fat, 15g protein & 5g carbs

INGREDIENTS
12 slices (12 oz.) turkey breast
12 slices Swiss cheese
2 cups baby spinach
1 large avocado, cut into 12 slices
1 cup homemade mayonnaise
INSTRUCTIONS
1. Lay out the slices of turkey breast flat and place a slice of Swiss cheese on top of each one.
2. Top each slice with 1 cup baby spinach and 3 slices of avocado.
3. Drizzle the mayonnaise on top.
4. Sprinkle each "sandwich" with lemon pepper.
5. Roll up the sandwiches and secure with toothpicks.
6. Serve immediately or refrigerate until ready to serve.

- -

'NEARLY' PIZZA
Prep & Cook Time: 30 minutes | Servings: 4
420 cal., 34g fat, 26g protein & 10g carbs

INGREDIENTS
4 portobello mushrooms
4 tsp. olive oil
1 cup marinara sauce
1 cup mozzarella cheese, shredded
10 slices pepperoni, sliced
INSTRUCTIONS
1. Preheat your oven to 375°F/190°C.
2. De-steam the 4 mushrooms and brush each cap with the olive oil, one spoon for each cap.
3. Place on a baking sheet and bake stem side down for 8 minutes.
4. Take out of the oven and fill each cap with 1 cup marinara sauce, 1 cup mozzarella cheese and 3 slices of pepperoni.
5. Cook for another 10 minutes until browned.
6. Serve hot.

- -

CHEESY BACON BUTTERNUT SQUASH
Serves: 2 | Prep Time: 40 mins
335 cal., 24g fat, 19g protein & 12g carbs

INGREDIENTS
1 tbsp. olive oil
½ lb. butternut squash, sliced
Kosher salt & Black pepper
½ cup parmesan cheese, grated
2 oz. bacon, chopped
INSTRUCTIONS
1. Set the oven to 425°F to preheat then grease the baking tray.
2. Add the olive oil in a medium skillet to heat to sauté the bacon, butternut squash, and the seasonings for 2 minutes.
3. After 2 minutes, pour everything on the baking tray to bake for 25 minutes.
4. Remove from the oven, sprinkle the parmesan cheese on top the bake for 10 more minutes.
5. Serve the meal while still warm.

- -

JALAPEÑO POPPER STUFFED ZUCCHINI
Serves: 2 | Prep Time: 30 mins
125 cal., 11g fat, 4.3g protein & 5g carbs

INGREDIENTS
1 oz. cream cheese, softened
1 zucchini, halved
¼ cup mozzarella cheese, shredded
Garlic powder, kosher salt & black
pepper
½ minced jalapeno
INSTRUCTIONS
1. Adjust the oven to 425°F to preheat then grease a baking dish lightly.
2. Place the zucchini on the greased baking tray.
3. Allow to bake for 10 minutes.
4. Meanwhile, take a bowl and mix the salt, mozzarella cheese, black pepper, jalapeno, cream cheese, and garlic powder.
5. Remove the zucchini from oven and top them with the cheese mixture.
6. Allow to bake for 8 more minutes.
7. Serve!

- -

TURKEY CARROT ROLL UP
Serves: 2 | Prep Time: 15 mins
275 cal., 7.8g fat, 15g protein & 3g carbs

INGREDIENTS
2 carrot sticks
2 slices turkey breasts
2 tsp. yellow mustard
2 cheddar cheese slices
2 tbsp. olive oil
INSTRUCTIONS
1. Take a plate and put the turkey breast slices then sprinkle with the mustard.
2. Arrange the cheddar slices then roll on the carrot sticks.
3. Put a medium skillet on fire the add olive oil.
4. Sauté the turkey carrot roll ups for 3 minutes.
5. Serve!

- -

SWEET & SAVORY GRILLED CHICKEN

Serves: 2 | Prep Time: 25 mins
175 cal., 4.5g fat, 30.1g protein & 2.4g carbs

INGREDIENTS
1 tsp. dry mustard
1 tsp. light brown sugar
½ tsp. onion powder
¾ lb. skinless chicken breast
Kosher salt & white pepper
INSTRUCTIONS
1. Set the grill to preheat at medium-high temperatures as you add some greasing.
2. In a small bowl, add onion powder, dry mustard, salt, brown sugar, and white pepper and mix well.
3. Pass the chicken meat through the mixture to coat evenly.
4. Grill the chicken for 6 minutes each side.
5. Serve!

LEMON PEPPER GREEN BEANS

Serves: 2 | Prep Time: 20 mins
91 cal., 5.8g fat, 2.1g protein & 4.4g carbs

INGREDIENTS
1 tbsp. butter
Crushed red pepper flakes, sea salt & black pepper
½ lb. green beans, boiled
1 garlic clove, minced
½ tsp. lemon pepper seasoning
INSTRUCTIONS
1. Put a large skillet on fire to melt the butter over medium-high heat.
2. Add the lemon pepper seasoning, garlic, and red pepper flakes to fry for 1 minute then add the green beans.
3. Add black pepper and salt then cook for 5 minutes.
4. Serve!

CUMIN SPICED BEEF WRAPS

Serves: 2 | Prep Time: 30 mins
270 cal., 22g fat, 52g protein & 1g carbs

INGREDIENTS
¾ lb. ground beef
Salt & Black pepper, to taste
1 ½ tbsp. coconut oil
1 tsp. cumin
4 cabbage leaves, boiled
INSTRUCTIONS
1. Preheat a skillet on medium heat then add coconut oil over medium heat then add the ground beef for 5 minutes.
2. Add the salt, cumin, and black pepper and cook for 5 more minutes.
3. Serve the cabbage leaves on a plate topped with the beef mixture and roll up.
4. Serve!

MAHI MAHI STEW

Serves: 2 | Prep Time: 45 mins
253 cal., 11g fat, 34.4g protein & 3g carbs

INGREDIENTS

1 ½ tbsp. butter
¾ lb. cubed Mahi Mahi fillets
½ chopped onion
Salt & Black pepper
¾ cup homemade fish broth
INSTRUCTIONS
1. Sprinkle the Mahi Mahi fillets with some seasonings.
2. Put the butter in a pressure cooker to melt then add the onions.
3. Cook the onions for 3 minutes then add the fish broth and mahi mahi fillets.
4. Cook for 30 minutes with the lid sealed at high pressure.
5. Release the pressure naturally.
6. Serve!

BROWNED BUTTER ASPARAGUS

Serves: 2 | Prep Time: 25 mins
315 cal., 27g fat, 11.6g protein & 9g carbs

INGREDIENTS
¼ cup sour cream
12 oz. green asparagus
1 ½ oz. parmesan cheese, grated
Salt & cayenne pepper
1 ½ oz. butter
INSTRUCTIONS
1. Sprinkle the asparagus with cayenne pepper and salt.
2. Put a skillet on fire then heat 1 oz. butter over medium heat.
3. Sauté the asparagus for 5 minutes then transfer into a bowl.
4. Put the remaining butter in skillet to heat until browned.
5. Add the asparagus, parmesan cheese, and sour cream.
6. Serve!

ROASTED BRUSSELS SPROUTS

Serves: 2 | Prep Time: 30 mins
202 cal., 5.3g fat, 12g protein & 12g carbs

INGREDIENTS
1 tbsp. olive oil
8 oz. brussels sprouts
½ tsp. dried rosemary
2 oz. parmesan cheese, shaved
Salt & black pepper
INSTRUCTIONS
1. Set the oven to 450°F to preheat then grease the baking tray with 2 tbsp. of oil.
2. Mix the Brussels sprouts with black pepper, dried rosemary, and salt then transfer to a baking tray.
3. Add the parmesan cheese and olive oil on top.
4. Place in the oven to roast for 20 minutes.
5. Serve!

MEXICAN TACO CASSEROLE

Serves: 2 | Prep Time: 35 mins
448 cal., 8.5g fat, 62g protein & 6.5g carbs

INGREDIENTS
⅓ cup cheddar cheese, shredded
⅓ cup low-carb salsa

⅓ cup cottage cheese
¾ lb. ground beef
¾ tbsp. taco seasoning
INSTRUCTIONS
1. Adjust the oven to preheat at 425°F then grease a sizable baking tray lightly.
2. In a bowl, mix the ground beef and the taco seasoning.
3. Add the cheddar cheese, cottage cheese, and salsa as you stir.
4. Put the ground beef mixture on to the baking tray and then add the cheese mixture on top.
5. Allow to bake for 25 minutes then serve warm.

- -

HAMBURGER PATTIES

Serves: 2 | Prep Time: 30 mins
488 cal., 27g fat, 56g protein & 2g carbs

INGREDIENTS
½ egg
12 oz. ground beef
1 ½ oz. feta cheese, crumbled
1 oz. butter
Salt & black pepper
INSTRUCTIONS
1. In a mixing bowl, add the feta cheese, ground beef, black pepper, egg, and salt then mix to combine well.
2. Shape the mixture into equal patties.
3. Preheat a skillet on medium heat to melt the butter.
4. Cook the patties for 4 minutes each side on medium-low heat.
5. Serve!

- -

KETO DINNER MUSSELS

Serves: 2 | Prep Time: 20 mins
217 cal., 11.1g fat, 22g protein & 6g carbs

INGREDIENTS
1 tbsp. olive oil
¾ lb. mussels, cleaned
1 garlic clove, minced
Salt & black pepper
½ cup homemade chicken broth
INSTRUCTIONS
1. Put a skillet on fire to heat the olive oil over medium heathen add garlic to cook for 1 minute.
2. Add the mussels and leave to cook for 5 minutes.
3. Add the seasonings and the broth as you stir gently.
4. Cook on low heat for 5 minutes with the lid covered.
5. Serve!

- -

THAI CURRY INSTA PORK

Serves: 2 | Prep Time: 55 mins
332 cal., 16g fat, 32g protein & 5g carbs

INGREDIENTS
½ cup coconut milk
½ lb. pork tenderloin
1 tbsp. Thai curry paste
¼ cup water
½ tbsp. butter
INSTRUCTIONS
1. In a mixing bowl, add the Thai curry paste, coconut milk, water, and butter then mix well.

2. Take a non-stick medium skillet and put the pork meat in it.
3. Pour the coconut milk mix on the meat.
4. Cook for 40 minutes while covered on medium-low heat.
5. Release the pressure naturally.
6. Serve!

- -

CHEESECAKE CUPS

Prep & Cook Time: 10 minutes | Servings: 4
205 cal., 19g fat, 5g protein & 2g carbs

INGREDIENTS
8 oz. cream cheese, softened
2 oz. heavy cream
1 tsp. Stevia Glycerite
1 tsp. Splenda
1 tsp. vanilla flavoring (Frontier Organic)
INSTRUCTIONS
1. Combine all the ingredients.
2. Whip until a pudding consistency is achieved.
3. Divide in cups.
4. Refrigerate until served!

- -

STRAWBERRY SHAKE

Prep & Cook Time: 5 minutes | Servings: 1
270 cal., 27g fat, 2.5g protein & 6.5g carbs

INGREDIENTS
¾ cup coconut milk (from the carton)
¼ cup heavy cream
7 ice cubes
2 tbsp. strawberry Torani syrup
¼ tsp. Xanthan Gum
INSTRUCTIONS
1. Combine all the ingredients into blender.
2. Blend for 1-2 minutes.
3. Serve!

- -

RASPBERRY PUDDING SURPRISE

Prep & Cook Time: 40 minutes | Servings: 1
225 cal., 21g fat, 3g protein & 3g carbs

INGREDIENTS
3 tbsp. chia seeds
½ cup almond milk, unsweetened
1 scoop chocolate protein powder
¼ cup raspberries, fresh or frozen
1 tsp. honey
INSTRUCTIONS
1. Combine the almond milk, protein powder and chia seeds together.
2. Let rest for 5 minutes before stirring.
3. Refrigerate for 30 minutes.
4. Top with raspberries.
5. Serve!

- -

VANILLA BEAN DREAM

Prep & Cook Time: 35 minutes | Servings: 1
205 cal., 18g fat, 7g protein & 7g carbs

INGREDIENTS

½ cup extra virgin coconut oil, softened
½ cup coconut butter, softened
Juice of 1 lemon
Seeds from ½ a vanilla bean
INSTRUCTIONS
1. Whisk the ingredients in an easy-to-pour cup.
2. Pour into a lined cupcake or loaf pan.
3. Refrigerate for 20 minutes. Top with lemon zest.
4. Serve!

WHITE CHOCOLATE BERRY CHEESECAKE
Prep & Cook Time: 5-10 minutes | Servings: 4
330 cal., 29g fat, 6g protein & 6g carbs

INGREDIENTS
8 oz. cream cheese, softened
2 oz. heavy cream
½ tsp. Splenda
1 tsp. raspberries
1 tbsp. Da Vinci Sugar-Free syrup, white chocolate flavor
INSTRUCTIONS
1. Whip together the ingredients to a thick consistency.
2. Divide in cups.
3. Refrigerate.
4. Serve!

COCONUT PILLOW
Prep & Cook Time: 1 days | Servings: 4
150 cal., 5g fat, 1g protein & 2g carbs

INGREDIENTS
1 can unsweetened coconut milk
Berries of choice
2 tbsp. 90% chocolate shavings
INSTRUCTIONS
1. Refrigerate the coconut milk for 24 hours.
2. Remove it from your refrigerator and whip for 2-3 minutes.
3. Fold in the berries.
4. Season with the chocolate shavings.
5. Serve!

COFFEE SURPRISE
Prep & Cook Time: 5 minutes | Servings: 1
55 cal., 45g fat, 15g protein & 3g carbs

INGREDIENTS
2 tbsp. flaxseed, ground
100ml cooking cream, 35% fat
½ tsp. cocoa powder, dark & unsweetened
1 tbsp. goji berries
Freshly brewed coffee
INSTRUCTIONS
1. Mix together the flaxseeds, cream and cocoa and coffee.
2. Season with goji berries.
3. Serve!

CHOCOLATE CHEESECAKE
Prep & Cook Time: 60 minutes | Servings: 4
230 cal., 22g fat, 6g protein & 9g carbs

INGREDIENTS
4 oz. cream cheese
½ oz. heavy cream
1 tsp. Stevia Glycerite
1 tsp. Splenda
1 oz. Enjoy Life mini chocolate chips
INSTRUCTIONS
1. Combine all the ingredients except the chocolate to a thick consistency.
2. Fold in the chocolate chips.
3. Refrigerate in serving cups.
4. Serve!

ALMOND CRUSTY
Prep & Cook Time: 60 minutes | Servings: 4
190 cal., 18g fat, 8g protein & 5g carbs

INGREDIENTS
1 cup almond flour
4 tsp. butter, melted
2 eggs
½ tsp. salt
INSTRUCTIONS
1. Mix together the almond flour and butter.
2. Add in the eggs and salt and combine well to form a dough ball.
3. Place the dough between two pieces of parchment paper. Roll out to 10" by 16" and ¼ inch thick.
4. Bake for 30 minutes at 350°F, or until golden brown.
5. Serve!

CHOCOLATE PEANUT BUTTER CUPS
Prep & Cook Time: 70 minutes | Servings: 2
450 cal., 17g fat, 2g protein & 12g carbs

INGREDIENTS
1 stick butter
1 oz. / 1 cube 90% chocolate
5 packets Stevia in the Raw
1 tbsp. heavy cream
4 tbsp. peanut butter
INSTRUCTIONS
1. In a microwave, melt the butter and chocolate.
2. Add the Stevia.
3. Stir in the cream and peanut butter.
4. Line the muffin tins. Fill the muffin cups.
5. Freeze for 60 minutes.
6. Serve!

MACAROONS BITES
Prep & Cook Time: 30 minutes | Servings: 2
125 cal., 12g fat, 2g protein & 5g carbs

INGREDIENTS
4 egg whites
½ tsp. vanilla
½ tsp. EZ-Sweet (or equivalent of 1 cup artificial sweetener)
4 ½ tsp. water
1 cup coconut, unsweetened
INSTRUCTIONS
1. Preheat your oven to 375°F/190°C.
2. Combine the egg whites, liquids and coconut.

3. Put into the oven and reduce the heat to 325°F/160°C.
4. Bake for 15 minutes.
5. Serve!

- -

CHOCO-BERRY FUDGE SAUCE
Prep & Cook Time: 30 minutes | Servings: 2
155 cal., 15g fat, 2g protein & 4g carbs

INGREDIENTS
4 oz. cream cheese, softened
1-3.5 oz. 90% chocolate, chopped
¼ cup powdered erythritol
¼ cup heavy cream
1 tbsp. Monin sugar-free raspberry syrup
INSTRUCTIONS
1. In a large skillet, melt together the cream cheese and chocolate.
2. Stir in the sweetener.
3. Remove from the heat and allow to cool.
4. Once cool, mix in the cream and syrup.
5. Serve!

- -

CHOCO-COCONUT PUDDING
Prep & Cook Time: 65 minutes | Servings: 1
225 cal., 23g fat, 4g protein & 5g carbs

INGREDIENTS
1 cup coconut milk
2 tbsp. cacao powder or organic cocoa
½ tsp. Stevia powder extract or 2 tbsp. honey/maple syrup
½ tbsp. quality gelatin
1 tbsp. water
INSTRUCTIONS
1. On a medium heat, combine the coconut milk, cocoa and sweetener.
2. In a separate bowl, mix in the gelatin and water.
3. Add to the pan and stir until fully dissolved.
4. Pour into small dishes and refrigerate for 1 hour.
5. Serve!

- -

STRAWBERRY FROZEN DESSERT
Prep & Cook Time: 45 minutes | Servings: 1
85 cal., 5g fat, 2g protein & 5g carbs

INGREDIENTS
½ cup sugar-free strawberry preserves
½ cup Stevia in the Raw or Splenda
2 cups Fage Total 0% Greek Yogurt
Ice cream maker
INSTRUCTIONS
1. In a food processor, purée the strawberries. Add the strawberry preserves.
2. Add the Greek yogurt and fully mix.
3. Put into the ice cream maker for 25-30 minute.
4. Serve!

- -

BERRY LAYER CAKE
Prep & Cook Time: 8 minutes | Servings: 1
450 cal., 35g fat, 12g protein & 25g carbs

INGREDIENTS
¼ lemon pound cake

¼ cup whipping cream
½ tsp. Truvia
⅛ tsp. orange flavor
1 cup of mixed berries
INSTRUCTIONS
1. Using a sharp knife, divide the lemon cake into small cubes.
2. Dice the strawberries.
3. Combine the whipping cream, Truvia, and orange flavor.
4. Layer the fruit, cake and cream in a glass.
5. Serve!

- -

CHOCOLATE PUDDING
Prep & Cook Time: 50 minutes | Servings: 1
430 cal., 55g fat, 4g protein & 15g carbs

INGREDIENTS
3 tbsp. chia seeds
1 cup almond milk, unsweetened
1 scoop cocoa powder
¼ cup fresh raspberries
½ tsp. keto friendly honey
INSTRUCTIONS
1. Mix together all of the ingredients in a large bowl.
2. Let rest for 15 minutes but stir halfway through.
3. Stir again and refrigerate for 30 minutes.
4. Garnish with raspberries.
5. Serve!

- -

POT DE CHOCOLATE
Prep & Cook Time: 50 minutes | Servings: 6
402 cal., 38g fat, 4g protein & 7g carbs

INGREDIENTS
2 cups heavy cream
1 cup Lily's sugar free chocolate chips
2 egg yolks
2 tbsp. dark rum
Food blender
INSTRUCTIONS
1. Heat a saucepan over a medium heat.
2. Pour in the cream. Heat until the cream starts to simmer.
3. In a bowl, pour in the chocolate chips, egg yolks and rum. Mix with a spoon, briefly.
4. Now, pour the mixture into a food blender.
5. Now, the cream in the saucepan should be hot. Pour it into the food blender and start blending it together with the mixture.
6. Blend until all the ingredients are fully combined.
7. Now, place 6 teacup sized pots on the kitchen top.
8. Carefully pour the mixture into each dish, leaving a 1 cm gap between the surface of the mixture inside the dish and the top of the dish. Cover the dishes in cling film.
9. Place the dishes inside your refrigerator and chill overnight.
10. In the morning, take out the dishes. Remove the cling film.
11. Serve each pot with a hot drink. I like coffee.
12. Add low-carb toppings of your choice.
13. Enjoy!

Made in the USA
Las Vegas, NV
20 July 2021